Roland Peelman

Anthony Browell & Antony Jeffrey

Roland Peelman

connorcourt
PUBLISHING

Roland, thanks for your generous spirit, your embracing heart, and your ever-exploring mind. We are blessed to have you with us!

John Davis, CEO Australian Music Centre

Anthony Browell and Antony Jeffrey have long been friends and admirers of Roland Peelman and his work. Anthony Browell has photographed him in and out of the Canberra International Music Festival many times, while Antony Jeffrey has worked with him at the embryonic Loud Mouth Music Festival in Newcastle in 2001/2 and subsequently as manager of The Song Company.

Their collaboration in this book is intended to give a portrait of Roland Peelman as he is today in the middle of an incredibly rich and varied life as musician, festival director and friend of many. Antony Jeffrey explains: "This is a book about Roland's wide-ranging achievements from the perspective of friends and creative people he has worked with. Roland has such vision and passion for helping create and perform music at the highest level, yet he lacks the ego that usually goes with success. Our hope is that his achievements can be celebrated by the widest possible audience."

"I have photographed many artists and musicians," says Anthony Browell, "but rarely anyone as expressive as Roland. There is a quality about his gestures, his movement and his facial expressions that seems to embody the music he is performing. I know of no musician with quite his intensity."

■ ■ ■ ■ ■ ■ ■ ■ ■ ■

The authors are grateful to everyone they have interviewed, corresponded and photographed for their readiness to share their recollections of Roland, invariably with affection and admiration.

Belinda Grieve's expertise, understanding and eagle eye as editor were deeply appreciated by both authors. Similarly, profuse thanks are due to book designer Paul Koller and production designer Cassandra Hollis. Anthony Browell and Antony Jeffrey also thank those who have lent photographs for inclusion in the book, especially Roland's family. The authors are grateful to members of the Board and staff of the Canberra International Music Festival for their help and co-operation. Most of all, the authors are deeply appreciative of Roland Peelman's time in answering endless questions with patience and thoughtfulness. Their one regret is that a few of his more caustic remarks could not be included.

Roland Peelman

Anthony Browell & Antony Jeffrey

Roland Peelman

First published 2021
by Anthony Browell and Antony Jeffrey

This Edition (Second Edition) 2021

Second Edition published by Connor Court Publishing
Pty Ltd

Connor Court Publishing,
PO BOX 7257,
Redland Bay QLD 4165
www.connorcourtpublishing.com.au

Text by Antony Jeffrey
Photography by Anthony Browell
Book design by Paul Koller
Production and finished art by Cassandra Hollis
Typeset in Sonny Gothic + Helvetica Neue
Printed by Shenzhen Candidus Printing

National Library of Australia
Cataloguing-in-Publication entry

Authors: Browell, Anthony, and Jeffrey, Antony
Title: Roland Peelman
ISBN   978-1-922-449-797
Subjects: Performing Arts, Biography

This book has been assisted by the
generous support of the Sydney
Supporters Group of the Canberra
International Music Festival

Printed in Australia

Contents

Roland Peelman
AT HIS FESTIVAL

The launch of the 2020 Canberra International Music Festival (CIMF) surprised everyone. Festival Director Roland Peelman decided he would liven up the announcement of the program for his 6th Festival by running a musical quiz from the piano. He would play excerpts from the Festival programs and ask the audience what they were. After all, it would be the 250th Anniversary of the birth of Beethoven. He thought it might even wake up the somnolent arts media journalists.

It turned out to be a riot of fun and laughter, (though sadly the actual Festival in May 2020 never took place due to the Covid 19 pandemic). Peelman is a top-rate pianist and a dab hand at improvisation. He is also a genuine entertainer and compered his own improvisations and the interactions with the audience. Anyone attending to hear a sober presentation of the ideas behind the Festival would have been disappointed. Everyone had a go at picking the pieces he played and risked praise or scorn for their efforts.

Then he introduced Eric Avery, fabulous Indigenous dancer and violinist whose wild performance drew whistles and cheers.

Dorothy Danta, former Festival Board member, tells of the "radiance of warmth and joy of music through the audience" at Roland's impromptu musical quiz. She says his great success at the Festival is because his process is all about the Festival, not about himself. Canberra music lovers "love him not only because he's a highly cultivated intellectual, but for his charming personality and informality with everyone he meets."

Another Board member is Swedish born Anna Prosser, who with her husband Bob has billeted Roland at their comfortable Canberra home for the last eight years during his regular visits. "Roland is a visionary artistic guy whom everyone loves," she says. Anna and Bob glow with pleasure when reflecting on the years he has been staying with them, now up to several months a year since he has been director of the Festival. He has a small suite looking on to their pretty garden. They laugh when describing how they might be in bed late reading when they hear the front door quietly click, the patter of quick footsteps to his room, and maybe the breath of some hardly audible music. At other times, he is always considerate, knocks on the door before entering. "His European 'delicatesse' always strikes a chord with me," says Anna. The Roland Peelman you see today is a very different person from the young man who emigrated to Australia with his wife and little children in 1984. The somewhat nerdish look of twenty years ago has vanished. He dresses casually, but stylishly. He speaks in public and privately with confidence and unfailing good humour. His erudition in matters musical is astonishing; hardly less so in literature and the visual arts.

■ ■ ■ ■ ■ ■ ■ ■

The lighthearted entertainment at the 2020 Festival launch masked countless hours of thought and assessment, visits around Australia and abroad listening to artists, negotiating with managements, balancing program options, all going back at least two years. At the time of the launch in late 2019, the May 2020 festival program was 90% set, 2021 was outlined and the following two years conceptualised. However, there is much 'twixt cup and lip: everything is up for grabs until the financial commitments are known and the major artistic projects defined, costed and artists available. The advent of Covid 19 and the virtual closure of the arts industry world-wide starkly emphasises the vulnerability of plans for a festival, or even a performance.

Festival Chair Bev Clarke says there are no less that nine iterations of the Festival program between its first draft and the final costed and

approved program. Roland Peelman agrees. It is not a question of the Board being unsatisfied; it's an inevitable, gradual process of testing and refining ideas.

"It starts in my brain in terms of an idea, years before a festival," Roland says. "Everything is up in the air; bit by bit it crystallises. I'm always thinking and writing: notes, articles, essays about the Festival. Then there's the puzzle about the artists, their suitability and availability. And the agents and co-presenters - the time that takes! By the time we go to print we are dealing with the eighth iteration of the program. The ninth version is the icing on the cake, putting the program book together, writing about the music and making any late changes and corrections."

Of course talking about high-flown artistic ideas goes nowhere without the income and funding to make it happen. According to Bev Clarke, roughly a third of the budget is raised from the box office, a third from government grants and the remaining third from donations and private sector contributions. As most Australian arts organisations know, the business of winning grants from Commonwealth, State or local sources is a fickle and frustrating process. Terribly time-consuming with outcomes uncertain and often contrary to expectations, it is the dominant feature of a scene where constant growth in professional arts activity is met inversely by cuts in government funding of the arts. For the CIMF it means the risk of expanding the Festival program (or prices or both) to gain extra box office and redoubling efforts to increase donations and win corporate partners.

She uses the words 'creative flexibility' to describe his method of refining creative ideas until they fit budget limitations. He regards the constraint of fitting the program to the budget as often beneficial: "It makes you think harder about solutions and sometimes the best ideas come this way." Former Festival general manager Alex Raupach says Roland is very attentive to ideas from others, whether they are people around the Festival or visiting artists. Roland agrees he has no mortgage on good ideas. "It is important to engage with the artists on a creative level. It is their talents and creative insights that make a festival exciting. But I have to show leadership about the quality, standards, context, integrity of purpose and financing of the program - it's not open slather." He adds: "It keeps me on my toes!"

■ ■ ■ ■ ■ ■ ■

Bev Clarke is full of praise for Roland's commitment and personal hard slog in seeking donations and sponsorship. Always a fine pianist, he now traverses the ACT and beyond with performances raising money for the Festival. It's a different story with the presentations to the funding agencies. She smiles ruefully when she says they have decided that he should not attend these meetings as it's not a good look when he gets impatient with the bureaucrats.

"He puts a huge effort into fundraising because he understands that growing private support is critical to our ability to realise our dreams for the Festival. His sense of responsibility to the organisation is finely tuned and he understands our constraints. Give him the budget and he will deliver on it, even if that means pruning a program, that in its early stages was bigger than Ben Hur. This is such an important contribution."

People on the Board, staff or Festival volunteers are intrigued with Roland Peelman's personal process before, during and after the Festival. You might call it 'Roland Watching.'

Everyone who has known him is fascinated by his ceaseless mobility - not just on the concert platform, but across a room, or from his home to his workplace. It is a kind of run/walk. If you were to watch him go from, say, Circular Quay to King's Cross in Sydney, a route he has often traversed, you might think he was walking very fast, or running slowly. However described, it is not especially energetic: he is perfectly relaxed and probably working out a program note he will write when he gets to his destination. He is not short of time or being impatient; he is simply using his time productively and getting good aerobic exercise as well.

Canberra Youth Orchestra

As the Festival approaches, this constant movement can be observed all the time. One of the problems is when his personal mobility extends to mechanical means. He is always getting lost - not surprising given Canberra's notorious circles. Anna Prosser and Former Festival Chair Arn Sprogis both have lent him their cars on the condition he pays the fines and excess on insurance claims. Last year he asked that these be deducted from his bonus. He thought it might be better to ride a bike instead of driving. He still gets lost.

Add ceaseless mental and creative activity to his physical mobility. At the ninth version of the Festival program when the Program book is being written and produced, he says that he has to move away from the planning process. "I have to turn to briefing staff about how to handle all aspects of the Festival, each event or concert. I have to think about how each event will look, what its effect should be, and does everyone know their job and

Bev Clarke at the Festival

what to do? It's about gradually losing control as others take over their share of responsibility. When it actually starts, I have to concentrate on what I have to do, whether it's greeting a visiting soloist or rehearsing a concert I am about to conduct. I'm not there to micro-manage. The transition from all the planning, listening and writing is stressful but it's good stress, not bad stress. The burden gradually lifts. The Festival itself is physically exhausting, but somehow relaxing."

During Roland Peelman's five festivals so far up to May 2019, the programs have become progressively more interesting - and challenging. The Festival's vision is broad and ambitious and each year a central theme or idea is explored; in 2019 it was 're-discovering JS Bach'. It also celebrated its 25th Anniversary with its largest program to date in 2019. The long-term aims are quite specific but will be hard to attain. That only serves to spur Chair Bev Clarke and her peripatetic artistic director. CIMF aspires to be a truly national music festival. Already it is succeeding with 30% of the audience coming from beyond the ACT. The expansion of the program to feature major components of Indigenous composers and performers gives Bev Clarke great satisfaction but she is keen to see

Applause at Fitters Workshop

greater involvement in Asian music, prompted by an adventurous Chinese theme for the program in 2017. She would like to see less Eurocentricity, but of course this is in Roland's DNA. Nevertheless at the next Festival he hopes to explore an extraordinary diversity of unusual issues ranging through female composers, Indigenous and Islander cultures, refugees, and transgender voices.

Less widely known than his musical prowess is his work as a speaker and writer. He writes illuminating program notes for most of the concerts, full of arcane but fascinating references; audiences love his pre-concert talks, often delivered wittily from the podium, apparently impromptu. His learned

discourses on music, composers or musical trends over the ages appear regularly in serious publications.

Leading percussionist Claire Edwardes has worked with Roland at the Festival and many other places. She sees his work at the Festival as "so creative …. his ideas are never-ending and can be so inspiring. He's completely immersed in the arts - and it makes something really special for the Festival, makes it unlike any of the other festivals."

Alex Raupach

Alex Raupach is the former general manager of the Canberra International Music Festival. He first played under Roland Peelman when he was engaged to play 4th trumpet for the 2013 Festival performance of Sculthorpe's The Great South Land. *While much younger than his Festival Director, they get on well together and he's unstinting in his praise.*

"Canberra likes an intellect: it's obvious from the way people switch on that they realise they're listening to a mind at work. It creates great currency, and he draws the best out of people. It's a process of seducing them to his agenda," Alex says with a conspiratorial smile.

"Roland is the hardest working person at the Festival. He hates wasting time. **When the Festival is starting - there's a rush of energy into a different zone, a sort of elation, high spiritedness, and he becomes very relaxed - high activity but in the zone.** He lives in the moment. He couldn't do it if he didn't."

Anna & Bob Prosser

Anna and Bob Prosser live in Canberra in a spacious house with a magnificent garden. For years Roland Peelman has stayed in their home for his many visits to Canberra. Over the years they have become close friends with Roland and regard him as part of the family. Anna explains that the Board has enormous trust in Roland's artistic decisions, and they all feel very lucky to have him.

"When he became Artistic Director, the company was going through a very difficult time and he had to make hard decisions about people and programs to make ends meet. With his amazing contacts around the world, and scrimping and saving, he did.

"He is a dear friend and both Bob and I often talk about all sorts of issues that concern us all. His family is tremendously important to him. He has four children, all grown up. **His eldest Jozefien who lives in Belgium, has three little boys whom he adores. He's a very proud and loving grandfather.** Two of his other children, Ben and Louisa, live here in Australia but Florian has returned to Europe where he plays viola with the best orchestras."

Bev Clarke

Bev Clarke joined the Board of the Festival in 2012 and has been Chair since 2016. She worked in the Commonwealth Public Service with a focus on industry policy for most of her professional life. She has also worked as a consultant and industry association CEO.

"Roland is a doer and he doesn't let obstacles or setbacks put him off course. He has an excellent understanding of everything that goes into delivering a festival and a great sense of the need to deliver the program on budget. He has a real instinct for understanding what our market wants. Roland spends an enormous amount of time with our festival team going through the whole program so that everyone understands his vision and expectations – identifying the special angles that will promote each concert.

"Over the last five years CIMF has worked hard to sharpen our vision and goals and identify our point of difference. Roland has been hugely influential in this process, particularly in promoting the work of female and emerging composers and developing the depth of engagement with Indigenous musicians in our programming. His contribution is significant on a national level, and there is strong alignment with the Board on CIMF's artistic direction.

"For each Festival, he does a phenomenal amount of work including fundraising – he seems to write most of the program notes on the bus to Canberra - so he doesn't waste a minute. **During the Festival he is everywhere, but still inexplicably hard to locate. It's always: 'has anyone seen Roland?' But then there he is, rushing to the stage, pulling on his jacket as the next concert is about to commence.** He multi-tasks his way through the Festival - announcing/ singing/ conducting/ playing. It all falls into place: he's amazing!"

17

Beginnings
FLANDERS FIELDS

Roland Peelman was born in rural Flanders. In his childhood, there was no running water in the bathroom, nor any understanding of his early passion for music. At age five he was given a toy piano that he played for hours on end. "My worst memory was being bored. I nagged my parents for a whole year to have music lessons.

When I was ten, I picked up my courage and knocked on the door of the only trained musician in the village - he ran the brass band - and asked him if he would teach me. He found a place where I could go after school and practice the piano: a community hall at the back of a pub. The memory of the broken ivories on the piano and the smell of stale beer will stay with me forever."

Instead of going to the local high school, he opted to board at a nearby town as a way of escape. The big event for him was his first experience of a sung High Mass in the school chapel. He watched open-mouthed as the red-robed choir entered the church singing. He was overwhelmed with the mystique and the sheer theatre. For an impressionable twelve year old, it was a seminal moment that sealed his love of music and theatre. A few years later he felt resentful at what he saw as being lied to by the Church. He rejected Catholicism but discovered Palestrina, Lassus, Handel and the other great choral composers; his love for sacred music has never waned.

His talent at the piano quickly emerged and after leaving school he secured a place at the Conservatory in Gent. Oddly enough, despite his talent, he struggled.

"When at last I could concentrate on my music, it became a complete fizzer. In hindsight, I was practising far too much and it affected my posture and health; I wasn't being challenged intellectually and I probably was infatuated with a teacher out of her depth." The turning point came under the tutelage of Claude Coppens, a gifted composer and pianist. He was immensely analytical and had the

Gent at night

demoralising habit of following the score marking every tiny error or articulation he didn't like. The terrifying rigour of Coppens' criticism helped build up the young man's confidence. Coppens made him look and listen to music in a way Roland had never done before. He insisted you have to know a score before you start to learn and practise it.

As a student Roland was influenced by older colleagues who were the luminaries of the early music movement like Rene Jacobs and Philippe Herreweghe. He became absorbed in the visual arts, architecture and various psychological movements.

Roland with Ben as a baby (Courtesy: Roland Peelman)

music, after graduation from the conservatory in Gent, he remained personally introverted and unsophisticated.

At the age of twenty-two, he married Annette Boucneau and they started a family almost immediately. Annette wanted to see the world and was the prime mover in the adventure to emigrate to Australia. There was also great concern at the time about the Cold War threat of missiles and the resulting disarmament movement, so escape to a new world was very attractive.

In early 1982, he was working at the Gent Conservatory when the director died suddenly and an opportunity arose to take a few weeks off. "Annette impulsively dragged me off to the travel agent and in March we were in Sydney with two tiny children and nothing but a vague contact in Melbourne. We arrived in the middle of a heat wave and a garbage collectors' strike. Imagine staying in a rundown youth hostel in Kings Cross with cockroaches everywhere. It was surreal!

"After two weeks, we were off to Melbourne to meet our contact and on the train we met an American woman who was going to Wagga. Soon after we arrived in Melbourne we got a phone call from the woman in Wagga who told us there may be a job for us at the Riverina CAE. They flew us all there and I was interviewed by the director (another Roland!) Bannister and more or less offered the job!"

To emigrate to Australia of course was a major hurdle. As musicians their skills were not on the list of wanted workers. They discovered this when the Riverina College wrote to advise they could not offer him the job. Annette was not to be deterred and returned to Australia in 1983 alone. With ingenuity and persistence she contrived an

The barriers were coming down as he became fascinated with contemporary music as well as the radical changing performance practice of early music.

■ ■ ■ ■ ■ ■ ■

Looking at the worldly Roland Peelman of today, stylish and articulate as he addresses an audience before a performance, the young musician who arrived in Australia in 1984 with his wife and two little children is scarcely recognisable. Despite his early talent and fascination for

Roland in Belgium (Courtesy: Roland Peelman)

invitation for them both to teach piano and violin in Mt Gambier. She took herself to Mt Gambier and helped her hosts through the complexities of the Australian immigration system. The upshot was they were told to go to the Australian embassy in the Hague where they passed all the tests and a year later the whole family arrived in Mt Gambier.

It would be wrong to assume he was the reluctant partner in going to Australia. Almost certainly he would not have emigrated without Annette's initiative, yet he was attracted to the idea of going to the other side of the world and starting an adventure with a *tabula rasa*. In Belgium he had already worked as Chorus Master at Flanders Opera, and just before he left for Australia, had completed a conducting degree at one of Germany's leading schools in Cologne. He had studied piano with the redoubtable Alois Kontarsky. But he found the music scene in Belgium stultifying, riven by the linguistic rivalries between the French speaking and Flemish speaking communities. 'Troglodytes' he called them.

They both loved Mt Gambier and their warm adoption by the musical community. Both became busy music teachers almost immediately; within two weeks he had fifty piano students. They were a novelty in the town and appeared on the morning TV show. He was invited to conduct the brass band and the local amateur Mozart Players. They both were thrilled with the embrace of the community but he soon realised there would be no more challenge in their lives in Mt Gambier. Later in the year he spied an advertisement for an Assistant Chorus Master at The Australian Opera in Sydney and successfully applied.

He never regretted their time in Mt Gambier. It had been a huge new experience and a happy time that brought them together with greater understanding. So just before Christmas in 1984, they packed their old Holden station wagon up to the roof with all their belongings and two little children and set off for the long drive to the big smoke.

Jozefien Peelman

Jozefien is the elder daughter of Annette Boucneau and Roland Peelman and lives in Belgium. She is a cellist and teacher and hopes to emigrate to Australia soon with her husband and three boys.

(Courtesy: Jozefien Peelman)

"With talented musical parents, it was inevitable that music would play a big role in family life. On free Sundays, dad would play the piano and we would sing children's songs. We would come with him to rehearsals…. there was no choice. I remember sitting in a basket in the wings of Sydney Opera House during a rehearsal of *The Magic Flute* with real animals; wow what a sight! What my parents did as a living defined how we grew up. It was hectic but very clear that my father was passionate about what he did and giving it up for something easier for family life was not an option.

"Dad has been a role model. Decisions he has made in the past haven't been easy on us as kids. But once I had to make decisions myself, I realized that his role has been important to me. Being a cellist - and a teacher - we do not differ that much and it gives us a lot in common to talk about. **Being together - whether with music or out and about in nature - is simply what is important in life. We enjoy our togetherness.**"

Florian Peelman

The younger son of Annette and Roland, Florian plays viola in leading orchestras in the UK, Europe and Australia, including the Berlin Philharmonic and the Australian Chamber Orchestra.

(Courtesy: Florian Peelman)

"My Dad and I have always got on. I can only remember him once losing his temper at me (we found a loophole in the 'No Burping' rule). We were quite surprised he got so annoyed.

"Anyone who knows my Dad knows how much Energy, Spirit, and productive attitude he possesses. When I was ten I started conducting class in Helsinki; it was my childhood dream to be a conductor. We played through a Beethoven symphony on the piano, him nerding out on all the bits and going over them again explaining to me why it's extraordinary. I wished more than anything at the time that we could have played together every week.

"When I turned thirty and blew my candles out, someone asked me what I wished for. I replied: 'to spend more time with my father'. In recent years the have played together on stage or listened to one another's concerts in Australia or Europe. **Those are of course moments you keep, when you can share what you love with those you love. It's what music and life is about.**"

Frank Nuyts

Frank Nuyts is a leading Belgian composer who studied at the Conservatory in Gent with Roland Peelman, where they became life-long friends. His study of Webern and other modernists had a profound influence on Nuyts' early career. Much later he became absorbed by the influence of popular and tonal music on the genre of new 'classical' music. Recently he has completed composition and recording of a long sequence of piano sonatas, one of which was dedicated to and recorded by Roland Peelman.

"Roland was the only student at the Conservatory who could cope with Claude Coppens [his demanding piano teacher].

"He has a unique ability to get inside my scores. I have never known another pianist to understand so well what I have composed, both intellectually and emotionally.

"His curiosity drives his insatiable search for new horizons. His talent is not just for music but for all the other arts too, and for life."

Frank Nuyts' wife Iris is also a good friend. She says: "Roland is always a breath of fresh air whenever he comes here, so cheerful and full of life. But he walks too fast! I think he will never come back to live. He loves Australia too much."

Roland with past Song Company members 2020

Ensemble

A COMPANY OF SINGERS

It was the first rehearsal for Mozart's *Don Giovanni* – I was about twenty- two. I came walking past with a score, a cup of coffee, a bottle of water. I teetered past him and said 'Oh sorry Maestro', and he fired back, 'you need a trolley darling.' Who is this man, I thought?"

Mark Donnelly, baritone with The Song Company for twenty-two years, tells of this first encounter with Roland Peelman, about to conduct Mark's first opera rehearsal. It says much about Roland's informality with musicians, his ease of manner. Shane Simpson, for many years chair of The Song Company puts it in another way: "There's a lightness of being about Roland; he rarely shows the dark side and is always remarkably positive."

While his informality and friendliness are the entry points for the musicians and singers he works with, his uncompromising pursuit of ever-higher musical achievement is the hallmark of all his work. The guiding principle since the time of the Gent Conservatory has always been that there is no limit to the excellence you can achieve, that responsive artists can achieve things with their voice or instrument they never knew they could. This is not easy for him as conductor, nor is it easy for the artists he is directing. Bass baritone Clive Birch says he was often driven mad by Roland's incessant demands to achieve the musical effects he wanted, sometimes for awful music, but the results were usually wonderful and he never enjoyed working with anyone so much. During an especially difficult rehearsal of one of his pieces, composer Ross Edwards asked Clive: "How do you do it?" with the simple response: "I don't know."

Roland Peelman's oldest friend is Frank Nuyts, leading Flemish composer and contemporary at the Gent Conservatory. They have boundless admiration for each other and Roland has commissioned and played many Nuyts pieces. Frank Nuyts was surprised when Roland, with his wife Annette and their first two children emigrated to Australia in 1984. Nuyts felt there were no limits to what he could have achieved in Europe. After a few months in Mt Gambier, Roland was engaged as assistant chorus master with The Australian Opera in Sydney.

Oddly enough, this was his first sustained encounter with the high musical standards he craved. "In Sydney at the Opera, I found a thriving and hard-working operatic engine behind the stage. Stuart Challender and David Kram were formidable staff conductors. I was amazed to see a schedule of twenty-three operas in my first year. I fondly remember all those operas I worked on with Stuart, and in so many different capacities. I was impressed with the company's stage directors too, especially Elke Neidhardt who was so smart and full of European theatrical know-how."

His own talent and competence were quickly spotted. He learnt to coach the singers in addition to his duties as repétiteur, and found himself doing virtually all the back stage conducting for the performances. On the debit side, staging of modern or Australian operas was mostly tokenistic, and he looked for ways where he could be involved in new opera. John Wregg was a house stage director at the Opera, and in 1988 together they established Sydney Metropolitan Opera, an embryonic company to commission and stage new Australian work. This was triggered by an initiative of Richard (Dick) Letts who was Director of the Australian Music Centre. He established a new program for contemporary opera and commissioned two one act operas. Several submissions were received but the consensus was that the outstanding project

Roland conducting ex-Song Company members at Martin Wesley-Smith's memorial concert at Sydney Conservatorium, 2020.

Peter & Martin Wesley-Smith with The Song Company (Courtesy: Peter Wesley-Smith)

was *Black River* by Andrew Schultz. The scenario was based on the major issue of black deaths in custody: a woman goes to mourn the death of her son and seeks information about what happened.

There was great reservation in the high echelons of the music community whether a subject as politically risky should be attempted, but Peelman and Letts agreed it must, simply because it was such a strong and relevant piece. John Wregg found an untrained Indigenous singer Maroochy Barambah to sing the central part of the mother. The six-month experience of coaching and working with her turned out to be one of the most significant musical experiences of Roland's life. Wendy Blacklock of Performing Lines found money to tour the production around Australia. The ABC helped fund a film of the opera made by Kevin Lucas that went on to collect several awards.

■ ■ ■ ■ ■ ■ ■

1990 was a turning point in his professional life. He left the security of The Australian Opera and within a few months had embarked upon two separate musical challenges, either of which could have made or broken his career. The Hunter Symphony Orchestra was a would-be full time professional orchestra based in Newcastle where the previous musical director had become ill and died soon after. Ostensibly this was the ideal challenge for a young conductor with Roland's drive and talent. The year before in 1989, Newcastle suffered the most catastrophic earthquake in Australia's modern history. There were massive casualties and much of the city's downtown infrastructure was destroyed. Local businessman John Robson was passionately supportive of the orchestra and felt it was a great vehicle for restoring Newcastle's mojo. Ruth Appleby was the manager of the orchestra and she suggested a fund-raising concert to help fund the restoration of the ruined Civic Theatre. She remembers: "Roland called in Richard Bonynge and Dame Joan Sutherland. Dame Joan had loved his work as her repétiteur and though she had retired from the stage, they both promptly agreed to come up to Newcastle and for Richard to conduct a concert with a whole sequence of stars of the Opera. It was a huge success." The musicians of the orchestra also had taken Roland to their heart. His expressive podium manner letting his spidery hands do the work of the baton delighted the players.

For mere mortals, taking the Hunter Orchestra to full time professionalism over the next few years would have been a splendid challenge. However, a new opportunity arose that Roland found irresistible. Back in 1983, Peter Seymour of Sydney Philharmonia Choirs had asked Charles Colman to direct a new eight voice a cappella vocal ensemble they named The Song Company. (Much earlier, Colman had founded the a cappella group Leonine Consort.) Seven years on, in 1990, The Song Company decided to set out on its own rather than remain a kind of poor relation of Philharmonia. Colman had retired and The Song Company Chair, Dick Letts of the Australian Music Centre, approached Roland Peelman to become the new director. Though he had never directed a vocal ensemble, a very different animal from a choir or opera chorus, he decided to accept. Roland says now: "I was drawn to the art form, my curiosity was awakened, and I had extensive knowledge of 16th century music and new music." All round it was the perfect decision: he remained twenty-five years at The Song Company, creating undreamed of standards of musical excellence and breadth of repertoire, probably unsurpassed anywhere in the world.

At the time, he was confronted with the reality of a massive over-commitment. He was paid a pittance by The Song Company and modest fees by the Hunter Orchestra. To make ends meet - by then there were four children to feed - he continued working with Sydney Metropolitan Opera and accepting conducting engagements with The Australian Opera and other orchestras. He admits now he was almost overwhelmed by the professional demands in the early 90s; it was only his razor sharp musical brain and his legendary energy that got him through. Eventually, he found The Song Company's creative path and growing international reputation was where his real passion lay. In Newcastle, financial problems and internecine arguments amongst the board of the Hunter Orchestra about its preferred role resulted in his frustrated resignation from the orchestra in 1997, followed within a year by its demise. He says now it probably could never have succeeded; the capital city orchestras were then becoming independent from the ABC and receiving increased funding while the Hunter Orchestra was left behind.

■ ■ ■ ■ ■ ■ ■

From his first days with The Song Company, Roland's resources were stretched to their limits. While he knew about the genre of classical a cappella vocal ensembles, Australia had no tradition of the type of ensemble he wanted for The Song Company. Previous manifestations like Colman's Leonine Consort, or Jones & Co set up in Queensland by Michael Leighton-Jones were successful models but their repertoire was predominantly early or baroque music. In 1988 before Roland took over, for financial reasons The Song Company had been reduced from eight to six singers. This not only reduced costs but gave the advantages of tighter ensemble and greater flexibility of musical style. In the early days it was a hard task as he had to find singers with the right potential and make heavy demands on them to get what he wanted.

He says now: "I wanted to prove they were a group for the NOW, with a clean sound and sophisticated style, able to do the hard stuff nobody had done much before. The first thing I had to do was re-establish its credentials with contemporary music; I like to be best friends with composers."

He explains that in some ways The Song Company was like a family. "You live together, you argue, you disagree, but you are completely committed to each other, for the common good."

Long-time Song Company baritone Mark Donnelly is eloquent about Roland's determination to achieve the highest standards: "I had never worked with anyone with such exacting demands and attention to detail, explicit in what he wanted. It was incredibly hard at first but it made me realise it was the career I wanted. He loved to push the boundaries of vocal colour in the ensemble. He took you along for the ride from the sweet sound of early music to a harsh folksy sound or absolute precision if needed. Initially he resisted pop music but he took that on too and started arranging popular music and loved it. He

understood our voices intimately and never asked anyone to push the voice beyond its natural limits. I always felt he selected singers as much for musical capabilities as for the voice. I found him a total inspiration."

This uncompromising attitude to achieving excellence can make it hard for those around him. Bev Clarke says Roland can become very impatient at Festival time with people he thinks are wasting his time. Claire Edwardes, leading percussionist and Artistic Director of new music instrumental group Ensemble Offspring, recalls a situation with an important recording being made by Ensemble Offspring where his insistence on recording personnel and process almost led to the project's collapse.

Anna Fraser joined The Song Company in 2007 and stayed until financial mis-management led to the Board's brutal decision in 2019 to discontinue it as an on-going ensemble and sack all the singers. Her remarks go some way to explaining what a tragic loss it is for Australian music.

"The level of detail and attention Roland requires from all his artists becomes like a drug for me (no other director requires it quite like he does). In technical prowess you have to be at the top of your game - you have to be in the know. At an emotional level he allows you more free rein - even himself as he's not perfect."

With former Song Company manager Eugene Ragghianti (Courtesy: Eugene Ragghianti)

"Then there's the issue of vulnerability. As performers, singers expose ourselves by this verbal communication we desire to deliver - it's what we do because it's the voice we've been given. The breath drives the physical, emotional and cognitive decisions we make. I want to be able to look into their eyes so that they can understand what I'm presenting to them. There's something wonderful about people engaging with that.

But for me a line has to be drawn; after the performance, I need to withdraw from that emotional engagement - for me there still needs to be a certain mystique about being a performer."

Perhaps because he is not a singer, Roland enjoys mixing with members of the audience after a performance. Unlike Anna Fraser he is happy to be quizzed about what he felt about the performance. After a particularly challenging performance that might have taken weeks to get together, he can walk away and set his mind on the next project while others will turn it over in their minds analysing where it could have been better.

The Song Company 2015 (Courtesy: The Song Company)

For Roland the intimacy of Song Company performances is crucial to their success, such as audiences of a hundred in Bathurst or Wollongong, or two or three hundred in Sydney. In this way he says you build up the audience support base, not only through the music but through people in the audience identifying with individual singers in the ensemble. He talks of another aspect of performing: "I lost count of the number of Song Company performances, thousands. But always the rehearsals were about getting to understand the 'why?' and the 'how?' of rendering the **music** itself, while the performances were about the seven of us (six singers and myself) **communicating** our understanding to the audience.

In 2014 Roland was appointed artistic director of Canberra International Music Festival, succeeding Chris Latham who many times had engaged him to conduct performances at the Festival. For some time he had felt he needed a new challenge, and with the CIMF appointment, the time had come to leave The Song Company. When he departed in 2015, he left an unrivalled musical legacy and a substantial surplus of some $300,000. He says little now, but it is clear he is devastated by the subsequent profligacy and the loss of a superb ensemble lovingly built ever since his arrival in 1990.

Anna Fraser

Anna was a member of The Song Company for twelve years to 2019. She is a highly expressive soprano and has forthright views about the world of music and the arts

"He's terrible at saying sorry. In all the years I've known him I've only ever managed to get two sorrys out of him, and I needed them."

When she was fourteen she had an experience at Chartres cathedral she never forgot. She looked out and saw the cathedral on a hill with the sun shining on it - it was a portent for later life. "I never expected it but there was a labyrinth in the cathedral. What I've discovered through my study of labyrinths is the process of finding your own path. A labyrinth is about a continuous single journey but because it folds back on itself you perceive your path differently every time you turn round the circle. It's about a journey towards enlightenment - like a higher level of spirituality

- and with Roland we agree we're all trying to seek a greater understanding of ourselves, the music and people we associate with and how we interpret that through whatever we do."

At the launch of Madeleine Easton's Bach Akademie, Anna ran into Roland Peelman whom she hadn't seen since he left The Song Company two years earlier. "I had loved working with him for all those years as a colleague and a friend. We spied each other and badly wanted to talk. But I had to leave, there was a sudden torrential storm, and as I hurried off, I found myself overwhelmed by tears. I realised afterwards that I had not grieved over the loss of Roland as our director and those twelve years that were such an important part of my life."

Clive Birch

Clive Birch was born and educated in England, trained as a singer and worked there in opera before he emigrated to Australia in the early 1980s. He says his English theatrical training gave him vocal and on-stage skills most Australian singers did not have. He joined The Song Company as bass in 1989 and remained until his retirement in 2014.

"I had worked with Roland when he was at the Opera and had been very impressed, so when John Grundy resigned from The Song Company in 1990, I suggested to Dick Letts, the Chair, that he should engage him as director.

"It was very much an early music ensemble in those days but when Roland joined, he brought in a lot of contemporary music. He always wanted you to go to the extreme capability of the voice to achieve the effects he wanted. But it could be sublime and he brought out in me things I couldn't imagine I could do. In a way my musical education didn't start until I worked with him.

"He loves the stage; a very theatrical person. I always felt privileged to be directed by him. His intellect is so far above everyone. He's a higher being.

I couldn't ever regard myself as a close friend, but he's been such an influence on my life in so many ways."

Mark Donnelly

Baritone Mark Donnelly grew up in Cairns and sang for The Song Company from 1997 to 2019. He found the job completely satisfying and regards that time as the central musical experience of his life.

"When I was trying to decide what I wanted to do after I had finished at the Conservatorium, I got a call from Roland. In a round about way, he asked me to audition - I had no idea what The Song Company was. I asked the manager Eugene what would the audition be like and what should I sing? He threw up his hands and said: 'Oh darling, something old something new, something borrowed something blue!'

"Since Roland took on the Festival in Canberra, I have enjoyed more open conversations with him than the working relationship we used to have. I always thought that his personal relationships were not a defining aspect of his life. He's happy with his own company. **He has such a full encompassing professional life - a passion for his business."**

39

Elena Kats-Chernin's study

Curiosity
PASSION FOR THE NEW

It is likely more Australian composers have worked with Roland Peelman to interpret their work than any other music director or conductor. Partly this is because he has commissioned or encouraged the composition of hundreds of pieces of music, but the real reason is his passion to bring to life new music of every kind - and to make each piece work.

He says audiences rarely have any idea about newly composed music they hear at a concert. Performers usually don't know much about the music too, he says, as they haven't had much time to look behind the notes. Surprisingly, he goes on to say: "Composers don't always understand what they've written either - not in a meaningful sense. Most composers can get a good sense of what they're trying to do after the first performance from the audience reaction. Then we learn something - from the audience, how the performers rise to the occasion (or not) and the composer learns something from how it sounds in the hall. Very often pieces are re-written after the performance. That's what it's all about!"

Many of our most celebrated composers revere the work Roland does with them to bring out the best in their work, often during the process of composition. For Elena Kats-Chernin, whose prolific output delights audiences far and wide, words tumble out her enthusiasm: "He will say, Elena, I want to talk to you about something. He's very direct and genuine. A couple of times I said Roland I don't actually have time to write a piece, but I'll do it as a gift. But you'll have to be here. So we would sit here at the piano for a day and create the piece together.

"He wants me at his rehearsals and gives so much time. Bar by bar, pulling it apart - and putting it back together so I can do some re-writing, getting the tempo and dynamics right. As a composer, it's great he gives me the platform to adjust such details.

"For me there are two kinds of people: one is the 'I' who has to find their own identity. The other is like Roland, who don't speak about themselves and want you to do something that's good for your own development, a bit like a teacher."

A good example of this casual but incredibly expert collaboration is Elena's version of a Stabat Mater that simply became *Mater*. Roland explains: "In

Eric Avery

2000 we had a tour to Italy and had to do concerts around Easter in churches for an Italian organisation called Women in Music. We were short of a piece so I asked Elena and she said 'You have to find me a text.' So I suggested the very Catholic Stabat Mater: Mary standing at the cross. She hated it. No. 1 she's Jewish, no. 2 it's a saccharine text, redolent of a particular time, and no. 3, lots of verses."

They quickly found a pragmatic solution to something that might have been impossible. Roland again: "She devised a really fast musical idea, a kind of riff and went through the text at 50 miles an hour. She wrote it really quickly and all the verses fitted in five minutes flat!" She reflects: "It's probably the shortest and fastest Stabat Mater ever written. Someone asked me how could I write a Stabat Mater in such a way - but I asked how can you tell me what grief is? It's a mother's grief. To me it was perfectly natural to do the piece so fast - because that is what is what grief feels like. It had to be very punchy, and has a lot of changing metre."

Two composers he greatly admires are Andrew Schultz and Nigel Butterley, both of whom have featured extensively in his work. Schultz first came to his attention with his one act opera *Black River* through the Sydney Metropolitan Opera production. When Roland arrived at The Song Company in 1990, the score of Schultz's new piece for The Song Company *Ekstasis*, was sitting on his desk and quickly became a favourite in their repertoire. Many performances and recordings of his work have continued over the years, most recently a performance and recording of his new music theatre work *The Children's Bach* at the Festival in Canberra in 2019.

Butterley has appeared less frequently but Roland's respect for his work is boundless. When he was directing the Hunter Symphony Orchestra he commissioned a major choral and orchestral work for the Newcastle Centenary in 1997 as he felt

Butterley's talent for large scale vocal writing was unmatched. Nigel Butterley delivered late and the orchestra's financial woes overtook the project. *The Spell of Creation* commission was taken over by Sydney Philharmonia who premiered it with great aplomb in 2001. Roland Peelman regards it as the greatest oratorio yet written in Australia, waiting for a second performance.

Ross Edwards, a doyen of Australian composers, speaks of his personality as the exact opposite of Roland's and how this works so well for their collaboration: "I'm the sort of person who happily sits in a room for hours on end and goes into a trance. I rely on him for quick decisions about my pieces - this energy for on-the-spot decision. It's exhilarating at his rehearsals; what always strikes me is the democratic process - he is an integral part of the ensemble. There aren't many conductors who have survived as long as he has

Simon Bolivar Quartet

Martin Wesley-Smith (Courtesy: Peter Wesley-Smith)

and maintained the adulation of the musicians."

Roland loves Ross Edwards' music and frequently comments on its apparent simplicity that belies extreme difficulty. The subtle gradations of tone and colour, not to mention the rhythmic intricacies, are hard to get right. A good example of this is his beautiful recording of Edwards' *Southern Cross Chants* in 2008 with The Song Company. He feels Edwards' *Kingfisher Psalms* of 2013 is an even better piece.

One of Ross Edwards' oldest friends and a fellow-student at the Elder Conservatorium in Adelaide was the late Martin Wesley-Smith, though their music could not have been more different. The collaboration with Wesley-Smith was possibly Roland's longest and closest collaboration with a composer. When he started with The Song Company in 1990, he was impressed with Wesley-Smith's children's songs composed in association with his wife Ann. About the much-mourned Wesley-Smith, Roland says: "I really took to

Martin's cleverness and craftsmanship. He was a great harmonist and knew about voicing. We really thought alike in many ways; he effectively became the house-composer for The Song Company."

In 1994 Martin Wesley-Smith and Roland took on a music-theatre project called *Quito* with his colleague John Wregg from Sydney Metropolitan Opera. Martin and his Darwin based brother Rob had a deep commitment to the welfare and independence of East Timor. Together with Martin's twin brother Peter they devised a theatrical piece based on the schizophrenia and brutal treatment in Darwin of a young Timorese, Quito whom Rob had known. It became a metaphor for the East Timorese struggle. For a plethora of reasons, including the late delivery of the score and the complexity of the treatment, it did not work well. Typically, Roland didn't give up. Neither did the composer. In the process of reworking the piece for radio, *Quito* became shorter, more direct and focussed around the music and the audio visual elements. It took on a life of its own. The ABC recorded it. During the years before and following East Timor's independence referendum, *Quito* became a touring vehicle around Australia and the world with Martin Wesley-Smith acting as a willing technician/operator. It was one of The Song Company's most remarkable successes, especially considering the stark and uncompromising scenario: a huge credit to the frisson between Peelman and Wesley-Smith.

No one understood Martin Wesley-Smith and his music so well. In a recent article in *Loudmouth* magazine, Roland Peelman remarked: " .... the essence of Wesley-Smith's creative insight [is in] capturing the enormous capacity of the human brain for rational deduction, complex articulation and broad empathy, through musical methods that combine the simple blues structures of popular song writing with complex associative mechanisms."

Peter Sculthorpe's *Rites of Passage* was presented by The Australian Opera for the opening season of the Sydney Opera House in 1973. The production was static and the music sounded heavy and enervating. After a few performances, it was mercifully consigned to oblivion. However when appointed Artistic Director of CIMF, Chris Latham decided to present a kind of retrospective of Sculthorpe's major works. For the 2011 Festival, he asked Roland to tackle *Rites of Passage* in its first outing since 1973. In accepting the task, he proposed to get away from the monolithic choir to a more varied approach with young people, children, adults, soloists and improvised percussion. "By re-imagining it with lighter more contrasted textures, all of a sudden the piece shone. The sound was clearer and the chords could be heard. I designated some of the sections to soloists. Peter liked it and went along with it." The result was one of the Festival's greatest successes, and a complete vindication of Sculthorpe's great work.

In 2003 Roland established a program called MODART that essentially was a series of training workshops for young composers in writing vocal music. It ran for ten years on a biennial basis; about 60 young composers participated, not only locally, but from Asia and New Zealand as well. Many benefited greatly from the experience and are now leading professional composers such as Katy Abbott, Kate Moore, Lachlan Skipworth, Tristan Coelho, Celeste Oram and Owen Salome. Roland says he was motivated by the fact that vocal writing was neglected in the music institutions and the craft was not being taught. He says he enjoyed doing the program as much as any of the young composers and no doubt he learnt as much if not more than any of them about how vocal composition works. MODART was full of lighter moments, such as Kate Moore's piece where each note was to be held for as long as a breath. It was meant to last ten minutes, but actually lasted forty!

Peter Sculthorpe (Courtesy: Sydney Conservatorium of Music)

Tambuco Percussion CIMF 2016

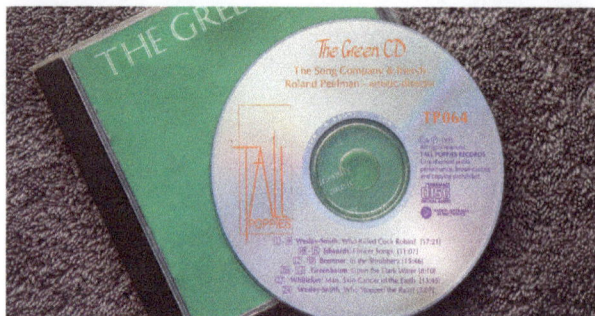

The Green CD, 1993

His fine-tuned ears and musical sensibility are permanently preserved in recordings he has made over the years. Many recordings of performances he has conducted have been made by the ABC, 2MBS FM or other music organisations. However the best are recordings made in venues in studio conditions, in most cases produced by himself. His earliest studio recordings were made by Tall Poppies, a fiercely independent Australian

Dan Tepfer CIMF 2019

label that has produced and issued some 250 CD recordings since its founding by Belinda Webster in 1991, most featuring Australian musicians with a large proportion of Australian music. Especially notable was the Green CD of 1993. It was based around Roland's idea to develop a concert program of music on environmental issues. The music was Australian and included vocal pieces by Martin Wesley-Smith, Michael Whiticker, Stuart Greenbaum, Anthony Bremner and Ross Edwards' *Flower Songs*, a work he greatly admires.

Much later he established The Song Company's own label and produced a series of superb recordings in the studio, most based on successful Song Company concert programs. As he became familiar with the intricacies of the recording studio, he preferred to produce the recordings himself in association with recording engineer Bob Scott. Some of the most successful of these recordings include: *Song of Songs* (Andrew Schultz), *As a Lily, Visitatio, Waltzing Matilda*, and *Kalkadunga Man* (featuring William Barton).

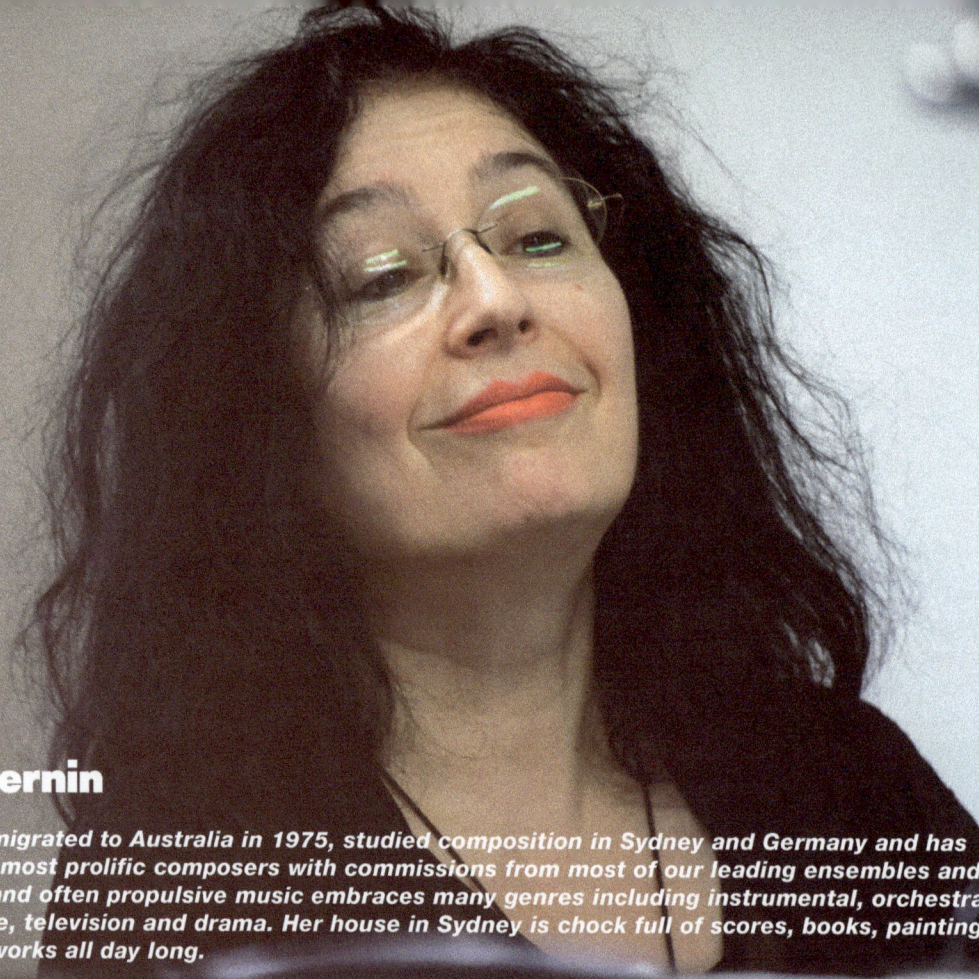

Elena Kats-Chernin

Born in Tashkent, Elena emigrated to Australia in 1975, studied composition in Sydney and Germany and has become one of Australia's most prolific composers with commissions from most of our leading ensembles and orchestras. Her colourful and often propulsive music embraces many genres including instrumental, orchestral, opera, and music for dance, television and drama. Her house in Sydney is chock full of scores, books, paintings and a piano at which she works all day long.

"My whole life I've been interested in meeting people who DON'T do what I do - who do something different - conductor, singer, performer. I find it fascinating what Roland does. I was a very good friend of Martin Wesley-Smith - he was my teacher, and I first met Roland at a performance of Martin's *Quito* at Rozelle. After the performance we had a fabulous talk about everything.

"He came to live at my house in Randwick with my family and I absolutely adored him living there. **He doesn't like to talk about himself much, more about music, his children and grandchildren. It's a different world having grandchildren** - it's a step forward over the first hurdle I call children.

"Who has ever done something like MODART? Performing and recording the work of dozens of young composers. Very incredible! He's a natural leader: has a clear vision and creative imagination. He's unlimited."

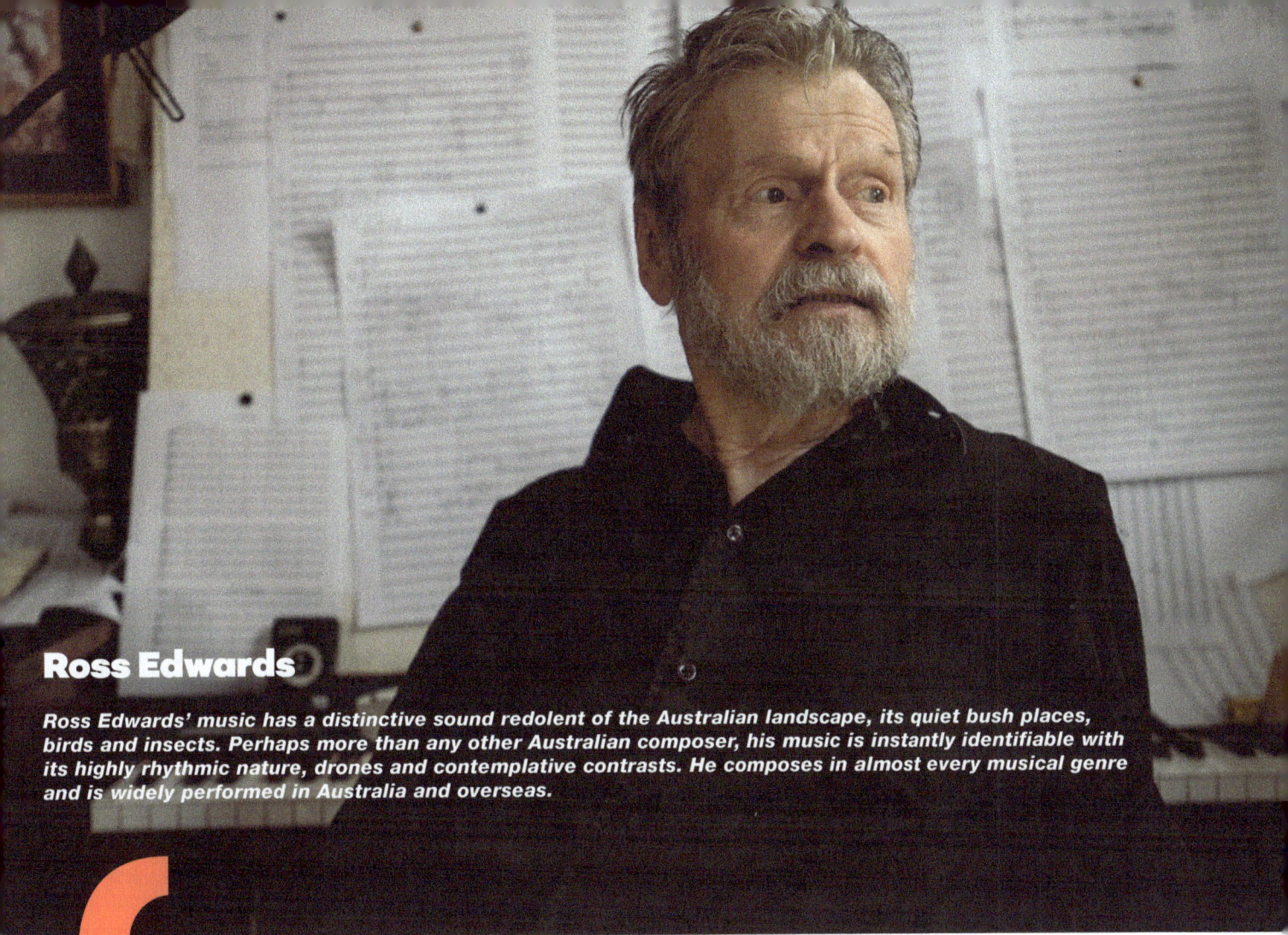

Ross Edwards

Ross Edwards' music has a distinctive sound redolent of the Australian landscape, its quiet bush places, birds and insects. Perhaps more than any other Australian composer, his music is instantly identifiable with its highly rhythmic nature, drones and contemplative contrasts. He composes in almost every musical genre and is widely performed in Australia and overseas.

"I often went to [The Song Company's] rehearsals at the Hunter Baillie church. They were obviously all enjoying themselves and all trusting him entirely, as was I. I was always grateful for his input as it was based on a total commitment and knowledge of the score and music generally. I gave them some pretty hairy stuff I must say - but they thrived on it. They were game for anything and it affected the way I wrote."

One of his most beautiful vocal pieces is *Southern Cross Chants*, set to texts by Fred Watson based on evocations of the stars in the Southern Cross constellation. "Roland wanted me to write a piece. I said I'd like to re-use a text by astronomer Fred Watson and not notate it explicitly. It turned out to be really difficult and I wished I'd written it all out. But Roland made no complaints. We added instruments and all sorts of things; we added William Barton on the didgeridoo, added percussion - and all along he said it was fine. No more SATB on its own!"

Peter Wesley-Smith

Peter Wesley-Smith and his twin brother the late Martin Wesley-Smith, were born and raised in Adelaide, the youngest of a family of four brothers. Peter is a lawyer who worked mostly in Hong Kong. In 1998 he returned to Australia and settled in a remote bush place in the Kangaroo Valley. A year later, Martin joined Peter after leaving the NSW Conservatorium, where he had taught composition for nearly thirty years and established Australia's first electronic music studio.

Peter and Martin became an institution in the Valley, Martin composing while Peter wrote his lyrics, and both organised remarkable musical and theatrical activities performed in the local hall, in Sydney and elsewhere. Roland Peelman became one of their most passionate collaborators. Peter says: "Martin credited himself with getting Roland to relax and get rid of his European stiffness. **He admired Roland from the beginning, always egging him to do different kinds of repertoire and take a more light-hearted approach to his programming.** Without Roland, Martin's music would never have been so widely known.

"Martin was technician and stage manager for the *Quito* tour with Roland and the singers. In Malaysia the consul-general said the video of the torture scenes would be unacceptable and must be removed. So Martin found some sheets of lighting gel and waved them around in front of the projector. The audience had no idea of what he was doing and the consul-general thought it was brilliant!"

Belinda Webster

Belinda Webster established the recording company, Tall Poppies, in 1991 and has since produced over 250 recordings. She has recorded a huge number of works by Australian composers, usually with Australian performers. Many of her recordings have featured The Song Company with Roland Peelman directing or playing piano. These include Martin Wesley-Smith's Quito, The Green CD, The Secular Josquin *and* Mozart Unexpurgated.

"My first project with Roland was *Mozart Unexpurgated* featuring Mozart's silly, and sometimes scatological writings. It was the first recording of these works anywhere in the world and good to get to know the irreverent side of Mozart. Another project was *The Green CD*, which started life as a good idea for a concert. It would have a lot more resonance today as it was ahead of its time in bringing together music that dealt with environmental issues.

"**Roland understands how to organise time to get things done. He has very sharp ears. As with all of the best musicians he approaches his work very seriously and with impeccable musicianship.** It was great to see him getting an Order of Australia."

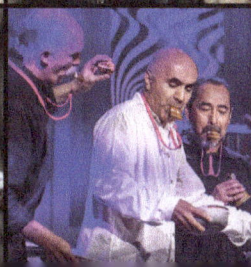

Conducting Canberra Youth Orchestra, Canberra Markets CIMF 2019

William Barton

Cultures

SEEKING CONNECTION

The Song Company programs were known for their great linguistic variety. The company sang as confidently in Italian or German as it approached music in Mandarin or Malay.

Roland Peelman is known for fine analytic skills in several languages while specialists were brought in for less familiar idioms. He once said he would like to program music from every century for the last 1,000 years, each one from a different culture. A pipe-dream no doubt. The fact remains that the music is there: the opportunity to present music from all ages and cultures to enlighten us is available, especially in the modern age when technology has such vast reach into cultural practices everywhere.

His prodigious list of composer commissions shown as an appendix to this publication, is itself an extraordinary, probably unmatched addition to music repertoire. It goes some way to satisfy his commitment to broadening Australia's cultural horizons. Obviously, most are from Australian composers, but composers from China, Singapore, Malaysia, Hong Kong, Philippines, Mexico, Belgium, Denmark, Italy, New Zealand and the US are included. While most of this music is vocal, the range of genres covers opera, ensembles, solo, a cappella, music theatre, electronic music, children's songs, and even popular music. He notes with satisfaction that more than 40% of these commissions are of female composers. His composer commissions were encouraged by Dick Letts of the Australian Music Centre and his successor at the Centre, John Davis. Letts saw an opportunity to build an Australian repertoire for small a cappella ensembles which he saw as an effective way to export Australian musical culture abroad.

A glance at the diversity of the Canberra Festival program for 2020 makes clear Roland Peelman's multicultural approach to programming. The most striking aspect was music by Indigenous composers and performers. Since his first visit to Australia in 1982, when he had his first experience of aboriginal 'dreaming' by accident in Wagga, Australia's First Nations people and their music and art has intrigued him. Involvement in musical projects came more slowly. He says himself: "One little window is opened and it leads to another." His work with Maroochy Barambah for Andrew Schultz' *Black River* was a big step into a new world. Back in his time with the Hunter Orchestra in Newcastle, impresario Andrew McKinnon suggested an Australian concert production of Gershwin's *Porgy and Bess*. The Gershwin Trust requires a production to be sung by all-black casts so Roland recruited a cast of Aboriginal and Torres Strait Islander singers. This project drew much attention and took place in several cities.

Getting to know Indigenous people was not easy. He understood the remarkable qualities of many of the artists, but understanding the people he met was slow and incremental; in his words, an organic process. He met with young didgeridoo player William Barton in Rockhampton in 2002. They had dinner in a restaurant and agreed to have a jam session with The Song Company back in Sydney. Nothing much was said and he remembers best

Véronique Serret

that the imposing Barton ate a large piece of Black Forest cake after dinner and promptly ordered another. The jam session in Sydney blew them all away. They had never experienced anything like it. "He is an incredible musician, with an amazing ability to sense how the music moves forward and how it is structured. He can play with anyone, an orchestra, a choir, any soloist or singer. From that moment onwards, William became part of The Song Company's household. We did at least one project with him every year." In 2009 they produced a handsome CD album, *Kalkadunga Man*, featuring William Barton as singer and didge player with The Song Company in many of Barton's own compositions. It formed the basis of an enormously successful concert program that was toured extensively around Australia.

More recently, Roland has established productive associations with other talented Indigenous artists. Brilliant dancer and violinist Eric Avery is becoming a fixture at CIMF amongst a burgeoning in-demand career. Composer Brenda Gifford has benefited from Peelman's practical mentoring in several ways. She was studying in the Ngarra-Burria First Peoples' composition program instigated by the ANU's Chris Sainsbury. Roland was impressed by her talent and commissioned her to write a piece for his festival, premiered in the 2018 Festival. She comes from a jazz background, and has played with James Morrison and Dale Barlow.

Brenda Gifford explains: "I didn't think of myself as a composer but Roland 'gets' the need to help Indigenous composers to find their voice. He will ask me to outline a piece and then workshops it with me. He really understands the cultural context. He identifies talent and knows what to look for. I was really amazed when he got me into Ensemble Offspring for a year's residency. Then his commission morphed into a recording." In 2019 Brenda travelled to New York for a performance of a new flute piece she wrote.

William Barton

From Harvest of Endurance Scroll: A History of the Chinese in Australia, 1788-1988. Artist: Mo Xiangyi, assisted by Wang Jingwen* (Courtesy: National Museum of Australia * See Appendix)

Percussionist Claire Edwardes endorses his facilitation of Indigenous music but has warnings: "We are all doing this for the first time. At first I thought - who are we to be telling Indigenous composers they should be writing in a certain way or writing Western art music, but in the end, it's their choice. There's no doubt they need these techniques to be able to have their music heard by a wider audience, and most have not had the advantage of university training in music. But there is a danger they get turned into overnight stars before they are able to express their ideas the way they want. We have to nurture, support and give them time to grow."

Her views are echoed and amplified by Australian Music Centre CEO, John Davis. "We've seen this over the years with his ongoing mentoring of emerging voices in composition, some of these relationships producing a body of work over many years. And more recently, his interactions with Indigenous voices, working collaboratively to clarify musical intent, to better inform performers, shape better performances that communicate with power and authority."

Michelle Leonard is a spectacular example of a true activist in opening up the eyes and minds of children in remote areas and Indigenous children to the glories of learning, playing and singing music. Her parents had a farm called Moorambilla near Coonamble in Western NSW. As a child she loved just being there on her own while her father worked the farm. She eloquently speaks of how she learnt the song lines of her country from revered elders, and of the 'highways of knowledge' that existed before her family came there. As she says, "The very essence of our world will change, because once you know, you can't unknow."

Since 2006, when she established Moorambilla Voices at the nearby town of Baradine, she has run an annual and increasingly wide-ranging music camp for children. In 2013 she invited Roland Peelman and The Song Company to Moorambilla as artists in residence and the ABC did a documentary about the experience. She says their work at Moorambilla was transformative: "There's something in the

Moorambilla Voices (Courtesy: Michelle Leonard)

vulnerability of the human voice that goes straight to our emotional core. Roland is someone who has sought to marry the disjunct that has operated too long in this country between art, through the hybridisation of voice, dance, music and the visual arts to what I call our connection to country."

Roland's fascination with music from non-Western cultures is probably best exemplified with his explorations of Chinese music. His interest was first tweaked with a concert tour to Hong Kong and China in the 1990s, when he says Guangzhou was just a building site covered in dust. "Chinese culture flourishes everywhere; Toronto, Sydney, Melbourne, Europe," he says. "It's part of our own culture now, so The Song Company had to embrace Chinese culture too. We learnt to sing Mandarin."

They toured there several times and Roland became familiar with several contemporary composers. For the Festival in Canberra in 2017, he made a major investment in Chinese music. He engaged important Chinese American composer Chen-Yi as composer-in-residence, and programmed much Chinese music for the Festival. The program included a big event at the National Museum featuring a large fifty metre scroll made by the Chinese community celebrating historical Chinese involvement in Australia, *Harvest of Endurance*. Seventeen pieces of music, vocal and instrumental, all from Chinese composers, had been commissioned earlier by Vincent Plush and Nicholas Ng, who organised the event with William Yang narrating.

On a light note, clarinettist Jason Noble tells of a tight rope situation at the National Museum performance of *Harvest of Endurance*: "All was going well with three works to go, when I turned the page and realised that my last two pieces were missing. Fortunately, I was the first chair next to Roland conducting, I tapped his music stand and whispered: 'I don't have the music for the next two numbers.' Roland turned his score towards me and I did my best reading the ant sized notes of the clarinet part from the score. But somehow the transposition was all wrong and pages out of order, and it ended up being some sort of all in free improvisation with no one knowing where they were. Roland was typically calm, gave me a good wink at the end, and afterwards claimed that the piece was much better in this new version anyway!"

Brenda Gifford

Brenda Gifford is an Australian Indigenous musician and composer. She plays the horn and taught herself to play jazz piano. Her composition has been mentored by Roland Peelman through the Ngarra-Burria First Peoples' composition program established at the Australian National University by Indigenous composer and academic Chris Sainsbury. Through their influence, she has been commissioned to write new works and given a residency as composer at Ensemble Offspring.

"It has been inspirational for a musician like me to work with people like Roland and the musicians at Offspring, and to learn their techniques for my own work. It's terrific that they come to my work without the Australian European blinkers.

"For the next Festival in Canberra, I'm doing a piece based on the four elements: sky, earth, fire and water to be performed by the Australian Art Orchestra, and I'm working with Liza Lim at the Sydney Conservatorium. This is great for me that I can have access to people like this as it's a new world for me, the world of classical music. He's a good bloke, Roland. He's solid and reliable and very supportive personally.

"For me it's about mutual respect between our peoples. Of course I want my kids to grow up to understand our culture and the struggles we've had since European settlement, but I suppose I've become more mellow over the years. I think it's very important that there's reciprocity between our cultures."

Claire Edwardes

Claire Edwardes is a leading Sydney-based percussionist and Artistic Director of Ensemble Offspring, a much-admired group of instrumentalists devoted to encouragement and performance of cutting-edge contemporary music. She has long been a friend and colleague of Roland Peelman who is a member of Ensemble Offspring and conducts the group for music when a conductor is required for larger scale or complex scores.

"Over the years he has conducted some of our biggest pieces. **Collaboration with Roland is always easy and there are no clashes with me as artistic director. He has a close harmonious relationship with all the Ensemble's players**……I don't see him as a highly technical conductor, and new musicians sometimes get puzzled reading his beat. He has a very personal style, very charming."

"At the Festival, he can get frustrated with the staff because he expects such discipline around all the things that have to be done, but at the end he always forgives and never holds grudges.

Sometimes he tries to do too much: at The Song Company he often used to integrate extra percussion into the singers' parts or for himself. It didn't always go as he hoped!" As an expert percussionist, she laughs at the memory.

"His music education in Europe has given him such enormous cultural and musical knowledge that's very unusual in Australia and helps greatly in informing our work at Ensemble Offspring."

John Davis

Founded in 1974, the Australian Music Centre is the national service organisation supporting Australian music. John Davis has been CEO since 1995 and has a personal knowledge of Australian music and composers second to none. All that time he has known Roland Peelman and admires his tremendous commitment to Australian music.

"In reflecting on Roland and his enormous contribution, there is all that repertoire that he has had a hand in bringing to life - the commissions, the premieres, the outstanding performances and the recordings. But less visible is his work as artistic director, curator, collaborator, mentor, thinker, and custodian.

"Roland has a heart that is driven by what is right, both in terms of art and social justice. Equity and inclusion are essential ingredients in his spectrum of musical expression. Working with Indigenous artists and marginalised voices is something he is deeply committed to. **He tells of some of the most profound musical experiences of his life coming from interactions with Indigenous artists.**"

William Yang

Born and raised in North Queensland from Chinese heritage, William Yang is a celebrated photographer and performer, famed for his photographic depiction of inner city social and night life. He performs monologues with slide projection in the theatre. They are a form of performance theatre and have become his favourite way of showing his work.

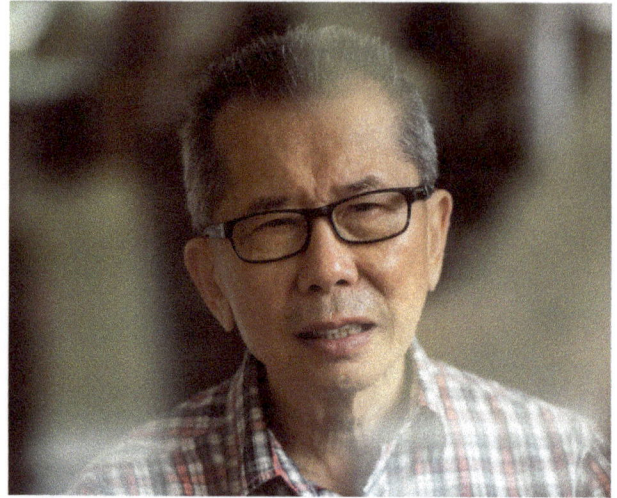

"Roland is a friend rather than a colleague! **When I got to know him, I realised he's an exceptional person, touched with genius. He sat down at the piano at one of his parties, and I remember thinking how music just flows through him.**"

At the 2017 Festival in Canberra with its Chinese theme, Roland Peelman commissioned a new opera by Hong Kong composer Hing-Yan Chang: "It was about a wedding and I was the narrator. I was amazed that during rehearsals he threw out most of the script. He was so decisive, even ruthless about it. He was right on to the essence of the piece and improved it no end."

Michelle Leonard

Michelle Leonard is a musician, singer and director of choirs. Her magnetic personality and passion for singing and the arts have given transformative experiences to a generation of children in remote areas. For fifteen years, Moorambilla Voices in north western NSW has led the way in connecting children to the rich cultural heritage of their land, and connecting them to the best professional artists and teachers. To date 40,000 children have experienced workshops to increase their skills with 300 per year chosen to record, tour and perform.

"In two generations where I come from, music literacy skills have been completely lost. This simply had to change. I was motivated by a sense of social justice - teaching music to children is a fundamental skill so vital in their intellectual, social and emotional development. Now we have professional musicians, composers, choreographers and visual artists working with elders imparting their knowledge to these children - the results are immense."

Michelle remembers the time at Moorambilla when she was heavily pregnant, then devastated by the no-show of their accompanist:

"Roland rolled up his sleeves and we did it together. And he was so funny! I was like a teletubby and he looked like a praying mantis. He sits in front of the children and they focus!

"I think Roland is an extraordinary thought leader because he is a real gentleman. I say that because he is gentlemanly in his moral compass, the clear artistic choices he makes and the relationships he has with all the people he works with."

With CIMF Orchestra greeting composer Gerard Brophy, 2016

Performance
NEW PERSPECTIVES

More than practitioners in any other art form, to be successful, musicians must concentrate day by day on their craft. Assiduous focus over the long term will always be the secret of their mastery. Roland Peelman's career has ranged over countless ensembles, orchestras, choirs, opera - large and small.

owever insignificant, nothing seems beyond his gaze. But this prodigality might be misleading. In the last thirty years his true focus has been overwhelmingly on work with two organisations: The Song Company until 2015 and the Canberra International Music Festival since 2009. It has been through winning the confidence of these two organisations that he has been able to focus his fertile mind on finding ever more creative ways of presenting music.

Much of his career has been spent with newly composed music, commissioning new work, working with composers, writing about and performing new music, explaining it to audiences. Not that he finds new music intrinsically more interesting than the great body of music from the past, but like anything new in the world, if it's going to be of value, it needs nurturing.

However we risk overlooking the fact that a great deal of his work has been spent with old music; music from the 18th century and earlier. The Song Company's base repertoire was always the baroque and early music of the Italian masters like Monteverdi and Palestrina, the Elizabethan madrigalists and the German and Netherlands baroque. This music is adored by audiences brought up on the transformation in authentic performance practice in the 1970s and 80s by the likes of Hogwood, Harnoncourt, Gardiner, Christie and others. Roland Peelman worked his singers tirelessly to achieve the highest standard in this music. As his colleagues attest, he always looked for new ways to present the old.

From his early days with The Song Company, he wanted to give musical representation of Easter in a quasi-theatrical way as he saw Easter as the most dramatic of the Christian festivals. No doubt this was born from his adolescent fascination with the rituals of the Catholic church. *Tenebrae*, the magnum opus of Italian madrigalist Gesualdo, had always appealed to him. It is a series of twenty-seven tortured chromatic responsories gathered in three groups of nine to celebrate the Christ Passion on Maundy Thursday, Good Friday and Easter Saturday. To present it dramatically, he consulted choreographer and dancer Kate Champion with the idea of presenting it sung with dance as a staged ritual. Gesualdo's music lasts over three hours, including linking chants, so they agreed it should be presented in three performances over three years.

Song Company general manager Joanne Kee secured the Sydney Town Hall as venue, an inspired choice. Roland describes the process: "The performances took place across the open space of the hall as well as on the stage, where the audience was seated. In the spot lit auditorium, all chairs were removed and in their place nine large painted banners represented the three sequences of three motets. During the performance, the light on each banner was extinguished one by one until a single light remained."

The most remarkable aspect was that the six singers danced as they sang this incredibly complex music, partnered and supported by three dancers from Kate Champion's company Force Majeure. Gesualdo's music expresses the agony of the Passion with laser-like intensity. The slow ritualistic movement of the nine singers and dancers to the backdrop of the great banners produced a unique and deeply moving effect. It was literally incomparable. The following year in 2006 the second group of nine responsories was presented within a changed but similar framework with Force Majeure. But it took another three years before the final group was presented; this time in

'Gesualdo: *Tenebrae* (Courtesy: The Song Company 2005 and Force Majeure)

Fitters Workshop

Carriageworks with Shaun Parker's choreography as Kate Champion felt she could add nothing more to what had been done in the first two representations.

Later Roland found another wonderful venue for his Easter presentations: the Crypt under St Mary's cathedral in Sydney. With its low vaulted ceilings and magnificent highly-coloured and decorative inlays on the marble floor, ceiling and pillars, it is a spectacular place for ecclesiastical performances, and boasts a rich resonant acoustic that can spell disaster in the wrong hands. In 2007 he arranged a 12th century musical manuscript *Visitatio Sepulchri* (Visit to the Sepulchre) that deals with the visit of the three Marys to the sepulchre where Christ has been brought from the cross. The Crypt, seating up to 300 people, was the perfect venue for the

mediaeval a cappella music that was simply staged with stylised movements and appropriate costumes. A superb audio recording was also made.

Another Song Company triumph at the Crypt was the great work of the 16th century, *Tears of St Peter* by Orlando Lassus. This work, consisting of twenty-one sacred madrigals, was presented with the singers standing in a circle with the performance given an exotic flavour by the addition of a Japanese koto.

As a complete contrast, the vernacular aspect of The Song Company's work was equally innovative. Early in its history they had huge mileage in the performance of Martin and Peter Wesley-Smith's so-called Barber Shop quartets, comic and scatological ensemble songs, usually send-ups of rural low life such as *The day we found O'Reilly's chook in Mrs Boon's backyard* or *Lines by a lovelorn*

cowhand. Years later, at The Song Company, Roland built a long running program full of contemporary and traditional Australian songs around the idea of *Waltzing Matilda*, and toured it all over Australia and internationally. The thespian talents of the singers were exploited to the limit, and the hilarity was lapped up by audiences.

∎ ∎ ∎ ∎ ∎ ∎ ∎

In 2009, when Chris Latham was appointed Artistic Director of CIMF, Roland Peelman became his conductor of choice for many of the major works in his Festival programs. This was not easy as a scratch orchestra usually had to be recruited from available players. Many student musicians were recruited by Latham from around Australia for most large-scale concerts through his Young Artists Scheme. Latham was ambitious in his programming and the task of recruiting adequate orchestral resources was aggravated by insufficient rehearsal time and a shortage of funds.

Nevertheless, there was no shortage of thrilling concerts Roland conducted at the Festival during the Chris Latham years. In addition to his re-imagining of Sculthorpe's *Rites of Passage*, in 2013 a reconstituted version of his TV opera *Quiros* renamed the *Great Southern Land* was undertaken though Roland thought it lacked a dramatic context. Most years he directed performances of JS Bach cantatas and in 2012 conducted the B minor Mass. A large-scale choral/ orchestral work *Eternity* by Ross Edwards was a major event. There was a great deal of Wagner and performances of both the Mozart and Brahms Requiems.

Most of these concerts took place in a largely glass-walled space in Kingston near the lake shore called the Fitters Workshop. It is a long narrow space seating about 500 on a flat floor with bright acoustics and a temporary stage. With insufficient rehearsal and sometimes questionable orchestral standards, the big concerts were hit and miss but the audiences were loyal and loved them. Roland especially remembers an inspiring Monteverdi *Vespers*. Despite a chaotic final rehearsal and a disorganised stage, he had prepared the singers well and there were splendid spatial effects, essential for the *Vespers*. It was a great occasion and the audience went wild.

When he became CIMF Artistic Director in 2015, Roland's first task was to recoup the finances which had blown out alarmingly. Large scale choral/orchestral works gave way to intimate presentations of equal importance, such as performance of all thirty-two Beethoven piano sonatas. Hildegard of Bingen's morality music drama *Ordo Virtutum* sung by an expanded Song Company for the first time in Australia was a revelation.

2015 was the centenary of the publication of Einstein's *Theory of Relativity*; Roland thought it a perfect central theme for his first Festival: "It was such a positive story of human creativity, a new explanation of the universe, at that stage not even proven." Perhaps prompted by the name Einstein, he remembered his life-changing experience as a student of Philip Glass's five hour operatic extravaganza *Einstein on the Beach*. As a result, a three hour concert at the National Gallery with Ensemble Offspring celebrating excerpts from Glass's best music was rapturously received by a capacity audience. His unavoidable choice of offering a small-scale low budget festival featuring unusual works of great power paid off handsomely

and brought finances back from the brink. With occasional exceptions, such as a triple quasi-operatic bill of Monteverdi's *Combattimento* and *Lettera amorosa*, and Pergolesi's *La serva Padrona* in 2016 and Handel's *Israel in Egypt* in 2018, presentations with large forces were avoided and programs became more intimate and exploratory.

Since 2015 there has been no shortage of showcases for Australian artists. Each year has featured a composer-in-residence, all but one Australian and almost all women:
2015: Kate Moore
2016: Gerard Brophy
2017: Chen-Yi
2018: Mary Finsterer
2019: Bree van Reyk/ Jess Green/Nick Wales
2020: Kate Neal

He says most were chosen to lift their national profiles and create momentum for their careers. He says: "It has made a big difference for Kate Moore as our commission got her the Matthijs Vermeulen Prize in the Netherlands, a most prestigious, biennial award. Last year Bree van Reyk gained a new commission as a result of the residency, and Mary Finsterer received the APRA award for best new instrumental work in 2018."

Besides Australian artists, he has introduced fascinating but unexpected artists and contrasts. The 2016 festival featured the idea of refugees. Gerard Brophy, as composer-in-residence wrote a piece called *Canticles* with references to pilgrimages, hope and loss. Forma Antiqva is a baroque guitar group from Spain comprising three brothers who made a big impression, as did Tambuco Percussion from Mexico. That year the festival included much baroque music. In addition to the triple operatic bill referred to above, he presented Rossini's *Petite Messe solennelle* in its rarely heard original form of twelve singers, two pianos and harmonium.

In 2017, when Chinese American Chen-Yi was composer-in-residence, the Festival theme was 'revolution.' It turned out to be very apposite as the Simon Bolivar Quartet from Venezuela was at the Festival in the week when revolution was upending their home country. Their stories at the Festival were very powerful. Chen-Yi spoke of her fearful experiences growing up in China trying to learn the violin during the Cultural Revolution. Another first in that festival was a remarkable presentation that has become a huge success and toured the world: *Stalin's Piano*, a multimedia performance with solo piano devised by Robert Davidson for Ukrainian pianist Sonya Lifschitz.

In recent years the Festival has become more professional and efficient. Box office and attendances increase. In 2019 the works of JS Bach were featured and the Festival was financially the most successful yet. Roland continues to provide both new and decidedly offbeat musical experiences for the enthusiastic audience. British scholar Benjamin Bagley's solo rendition of the Old English masterpiece *Beowulf* was electrifying. The platform he gave for three years (2017-19) to Bach Akademie, a new orchestra founded by young Australian baroque violinist Madeleine Easton, was not only far-sighted but benefited both Bach Akademie and the Festival.

Ella Macens

Ella Macens is one of Australia's most sought after younger composers. She was one of four composers selected to participate in the Sydney Conservatorium of Music's inaugural National Women Composers' Development Program (2016-17), and has recently completed a two year composer residency at the Sydney Children's Choir. She teaches composition at the Sydney Conservatorium and Sydney University. Heavily influenced by her Latvian heritage, Ella grew up in a rich and colourful community surrounded by instrumental folk music, baltic choral music and traditional dance.

Ella was approached by Roland Peelman in 2018 to compose a new work for the Sonic Art Saxophone Quartet. She explains the experience of their first meeting:

"Roland invited me over for coffee to discuss the commission. His enthusiasm surrounding the project was really inspiring! I was a bit nervous because I had never composed for saxophone before. He knew of my Latvian heritage and connection with choral music, and explained that composing for saxophone quartet is very similar to composing for voices. He shared some examples of his favourite saxophone quartet works with me, and encouraged me to ask him questions along the way. That's how I treated the new work - as a piece for four distinct voices that can both blur into one unified sound, and separate into moments of distinct clarity and variation."

Shane Simpson

Founder of arts law firm Simpsons, long time Chair of The Song Company until 2010 and indefatigable facilitator and consumer of the arts, Shane Simpson has been a close colleague of Roland Peelman for many years. No one has more expert knowledge of the needs of artists and arts organisations to allow them to survive and flourish.

"Roland brought The Song Company to sing the Victoria Mass at my mother's funeral. I thought it was an act of such kindness and generosity.

"Once we were financially in a very tight corner at The Song Company. The Board, Roland and the singers discussed options to survive like reducing the programs. What really surprised us was the singers and Roland came back with an offer to take a pay cut. It showed such a strong commitment, especially as we all had been wanting to increase their inadequate salaries.

He's unwavering in his enthusiasm and advocacy for the 'idea' ... I was delighted with his progression from the 'interior' type of existence at The Song Company to a festival with such artistic scope. It may not come naturally to him, but now he has to be a net-worker." Simpson believes the festival will need to use its natural advantages if it is to fulfil its ambition to be a genuinely national festival. "It's not easy - but Canberra has all the levers necessary – politicians, top bureaucrats, as well as leaders of industry associations and union groups."

Richard Letts

Richard (Dick) Letts runs his own foundation, The Music Trust, dedicated to the propagation of Australian music and musical talent. He is Chair of Symphony for Life, a project to introduce underprivileged children to playing orchestral instruments. Most of his life he has worked tirelessly for Australian music, first as director of the Australia Council Music Board and later for the Australian Music Centre. He founded and directed the National Music Council for a long period, and was Chair of The Song Company for twelve years.

"He has such expressive hands when he's directing. I feel a bit outclassed by Roland's musical knowledge. I've often had him as a judge at the Freedman Fellowships which I organise. Though the process of listening to nominees and ranking is done by each judge before they meet, **I often find Roland's choice is the same as the panel's collective choice.**

"The popular music he did with The Song Company when I was on the Board no doubt appealed to the audience we had, but I thought it wasn't the sort of music that would appeal to younger audiences, and it's those audiences that we should be reaching."

Ken Unsworth

Ken Unsworth is an artist of many parts, who for over sixty years, has followed his own often controversial path as visual artist, sculptor, poet, performer and creator of large scale art installations. His late wife Elisabeth was a pianist, his collaborator and muse. Much of his work reflects her presence and inspiration. Roland Peelman often visits him at home and enjoys playing Ken's Steinway and talking at length about art, politics and the world.

Roland has been involved in several of Ken Unsworth's installations. On asked whether he enjoys collaboration with Roland, he says: "I only collaborate by necessity. For music I talk to the composer for what I want to do - so far it's worked. I'm essentially egotistical and selfish. I need to have control over my work. I outline the work and fill in a lot of the details and it comes to a point when you say take it and do what you have to do. Sometimes it doesn't work as much as I'd like it to.

"Roland is an artist out of the mainstream, so good at what he does. Like most of the best artists, he is fully aware of what's going on in the world around him and is very approachable.

"In one installation, I put him in top hat, tails and white gloves and he brought people into the room. He was wonderful."

Florian Peelman and Roland at CIMF 2017

Life at large

FAMILY, FRIENDS & ADVENTURE

For years Roland Peelman has spent his Australian summer holidays in isolated places like the Tasmanian wilderness, usually with members of his family or friends. It's a time to get away from crowds, relax and rejuvenate.

Now in his early sixties, he is very fit and strong with not an ounce of extra flesh. Late in 2019, he spent a couple of weeks with his son Florian tramping and climbing around the Dolomites. Exhausting for any young person, Roland hardly drew breath the whole time. His daughter Jozefien recalls outdoor holidays as being a big part of her life. "Family holidays meant walking! It was always clear that Dad would either walk or bike wherever he is; holidays in France, Austria, Corsica - it's all walking, usually in worn-out old sneakers. My three kids love it. As long as there is no time schedule all is fine. We've only had to rescue him once!" Quite independently, Florian tells of his father's apparent determination to wear out old sneakers on these hazardous excursions.

One of Roland's first outdoor experiences when he arrived in Australia was a camping trip to Wilson's Promontory. It opened his eyes to the wonder of the Australian landscape. Even more powerful was the **smell** of the country and the bush when he travelled briefly to Wagga on his first visit in 1982. He had never smelt anything like it before and that perception has never left him.

It's tempting to conflate his love of the wild and of artistic discovery with the Romantic ideals of the first half of the 19th century. Caspar David Friedrich's famous painting *Wanderer in a Sea of Fog* comes to mind where the frock-coated young man stands on a crag contemplating the sublime landscape set out before him. This would be a mistake. He is nothing if not an intensely practical down to earth man who has little time for hazy romantic notions. His holidays in the wild are about companionship and relaxation. They are essential breaks from a highly organised professional life where not a moment is wasted, even if it's to go to a party he wants to attend.

His lifestyle puzzles many people who don't know him well. He doesn't own a house or apartment; he

With Tom Jones

Jozefien (on phone)

Celebrating Order of Australia Award

doesn't even rent an abode. He doesn't drink wine like most of his friends: he drinks beer. In Sydney for years he has lived as a guest in the Glebe house of Pattie Benjamin. The same applies to his time in Canberra where he stays at the home of Anna and Bob Prosser. He doesn't own a car and takes public transport wherever he can't walk, including the frequent journeys by bus to and from Canberra. He possesses virtually no domestic paraphernalia apart from his scores, books, laptop and clothes.

Shane Simpson, for many years Chair of The Song Company, ruminates that "his lifestyle is like a monk devoted to the Lord, except he's devoted to music." This might be a mistake too as his lifestyle is not monkish and he is very sociable, moving amongst many interesting and talented friends. He seems perfectly content with this minimalist existence. It frees him from most of the domestic chores and responsibilities that weigh down people's daily lives. On the other hand, part of the austerity is no doubt dictated by ludicrously low remuneration he has received most of his life from the cash-starved organisations he has worked for. While he never complains about this, the CIMF is well aware of the need to pay more for a man of his stature

though the devastating effect of the pandemic on the livelihoods of musicians and artists everywhere makes this a pipe dream.

Anna Prosser has a slightly different take on the way he lives his life, saying: "We never talk about his intimate relationships, but then I think these days he has little or no time for intimate relationships. He sublimates most of his emotional life into his music and artistic interests and to the artists he works with." A typical example of this generosity took place at the launch event of the 2020 Festival late in 2019. He had been very impressed with the talent of Indigenous violinist and dancer Eric Avery and invited him to give a brief performance at the Festival launch. The mercurial Avery (Michelle Leonard eloquently describes him as 'floating like smoke') was fast becoming a celebrity and had been invited to meet and play with visiting star cellist Yo Yo Ma. Roland picked Eric up from the bus, organised to have his violin glued, ironed Eric's clothes and after the launch, hired a car and drove Eric back to Sydney for his appointment with the great man.

■ ■ ■ ■ ■ ■ ■

With Florian and Lauren in the Dolomites (Courtesy: Florian Peelman)

Arriving in Mt Gambier in 1984, Roland by his own admission was bookish and naive, unprepared for life's hurly burly. "Being obsessed as I was by music and the arts, I did not realise how it can take over your life and sublimate the day to day reality. I think on a personal level I was very repressed and un-free. Though I don't for a moment regret my marriage or the wonderful offspring it has given me, I have to admit I was too young and wasn't ready to be a husband or being a good family man. At some point I had to come to terms with who I really was."

When they moved to Sydney, he was flung into the raffish bohemian life back stage at The Australian Opera. Like Candide, he was an ingenue starting a new adventure. A few years later in 1990, Eugene Ragghianti became manager of The Song Company for the first decade of Roland Peelman's artistic directorship. He has spent his life in the music and entertainment business and was the ideal tutor for showing a serious minded European-educated musician the way to get along in the byways of the Australian musical scene.

"When I got the job, he was rather stitched up with me, very correct," confides Ragghianti, "but I soon brought him round and taught him an Australian sense of humour. After all, I had worked in music hall, so I had to explain the Australian idiom. I remember I once said to him, 'you'll have to write the blurb for the next concert', and he said, 'what is blurb?' At that time he was spending most of his time travelling everywhere with The Song Company or in Newcastle with the Hunter Orchestra. He was starting to come out but his wife and family were on the North Shore and I had the impression she didn't know."

In Newcastle, the pattern of billeting with friendly families started. Ruth Appleby was appointed manager of the Hunter Orchestra shortly before he took up the position as musical director. She and her husband Steve had a big house and she liked him so much she invited him to live with them. He accepted without hesitation. Newcastle was a different experience again. The musicians loved working with him. He was accepted with open arms into the broader Newcastle community and at first it gave him a break from the unresolved conundrum of his marriage and life in Sydney.

The marriage with Annette broke up in 1991. After a few years of constant travel, (including a six-month trip around Australia in a Kombi-van), she resettled in Finland where all four children were educated. A few years later in Sydney, he met and started a relationship with a man much younger than himself, Tom Jones, who remembers: "I was a wide eyed undergrad with my own amateur passion for classical music and so was somewhat star-struck by this charming Belgian conductor."

It was an easy and companionable partnership for them both and perhaps the first mature loving relationship in Roland's life. Tom Jones fitted in easily with the Song Company singers whose lives were intertwined because of the constant touring. In some ways it was the first time that he had lived a secure and settled home life since moving to Australia. But the professional demands on his life never made the relationship simple. Tom Jones says: "There was always an extra tenant that had to be accommodated – his baby grand... of course when someone is as committed to their work as Roland, it inevitably had a knock-on effect. The travel and long periods apart were a great challenge. Unfortunately, the travel, money, the demands of parenthood of his children all proved too much for me to handle. I found myself starting to live in his shadow so I had to make a choice." After a number of years they both found themselves drifting apart and the relationship came to an amicable end.

Roland's mindset was changing too. His commitment to his professional life increasingly took over his whole life. Deep down this was what he wanted. Committing to a full-time loving partnership was psychologically secondary, a recipe for failure. His wide-ranging friendships gave him a great deal of support and much pleasure. As his children grew up, two came to live in Australia, a development that delighted him and led over the years to deeper relations with them all. Now that his children are all adults, he has got to know them well, has worked at the relationships from their aspects as well as his own, though it has not all been plain sailing. Many of his friends testify to his pride in his children and presence in their lives. Though his grandchildren still live in Belgium, he adores them and is in constant FaceTime touch.

All this is not to say he has retreated to a celibate existence; his passion to explore unfamiliar places and people led to a highly charged liaison in Mexico that survived a few years of meetings in Mexico and elsewhere. There is no prospect of his energy diminishing or settling down to a more comfortable existence.

With Tom Jones and Eugene Ragghianti (Courtesy: Eugene Ragghianti)

Playing for friends

Sandy Belford

Sandy Belford was a partner in a leading branding and graphic art agency, Principals, which provided support in style strategy and design to The Song Company for many years. He always felt a Song Company performance was like a mini festival, always with some interesting or surprising perspective.

"I suspect the singers loved his novel approach to any concert - that whatever they were going to do it wasn't just going to be standing on the stage.

"I've often thought he should be on TV - I don't think I've ever had a conversation with him that he doesn't know something about. He can talk about anything at all.

"For the Festival there he is charging around the world. I can see him utterly in his element. I'm hoping he will stay at Canberra for a few more years, as it's spot on - it's got momentum though not obvious where he would go after this in Australia. He is a national asset, but I suspect his quirky personality might be out of synch with the major arts organisations.."

Eugene Ragghianti

Eugene Ragghianti comes from an Italo-Australian family and now lives in Adelaide. From 1991, he spent ten years as general manager of The Song Company. His avuncular geniality with everyone was legendary. He had an irrepressible habit of selling tickets or raising donations with anyone he met, like a virtual door to door salesman.

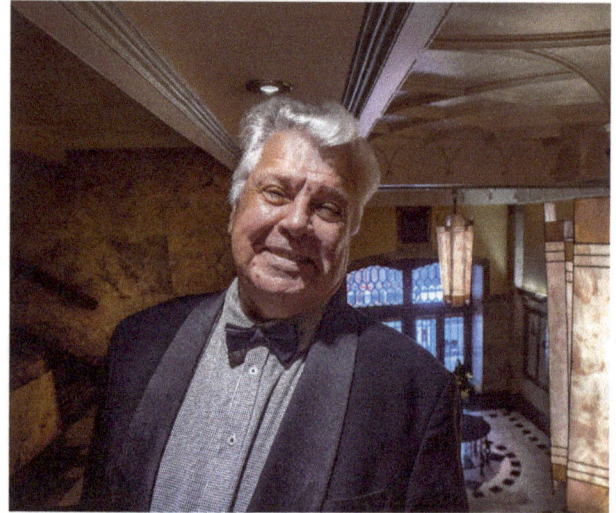

"The very first concert we did under my management was *A Green Concert* in 1991 at the Sydney Opera House concert hall in reverse mode where the singers stood downstage facing towards the audience in the choir seats. It was based on environmental issues and included four world premieres.

"In those days it was terribly hard work: we did commercial gigs, shopping centres, jingles, cabaret shows, all just to make ends meet.

"He could be very dogmatic in rehearsal with the singers, extremely strict. I was amused at a remark made by a frustrated singer who said the Belgians were worse than the Germans in WW2. However to be fair, as the singers became more experienced and got to know what he wanted he became more mellow."

Amy Curl

Amy Curl is an expert in arts marketing and social media management. In 2010 she joined The Song Company and worked there for several years during Roland Peelman's time as Artistic Director. She and Roland became firm friends despite their totally different musical backgrounds. She has a pop music and jazz background and later ran SIMA (Sydney Improvised Music Association).

"When I first saw Roland conduct a Song Company concert, he extended those arms - I'd never seen a pair of arms go so wide. I thought to myself, this is a man in the right job - those arms are born to conduct. And those incredible hands: the way he decorates and illustrates the music with his hands.

"It was easy to discuss marketing ideas with him. He was never anxious to get away - he was very much part of the process. That's what I loved about working with Roland - he was engaged at any level as much or as little he needed to be.

"I actually noticed his clothes last Saturday night. Very funky and next stage: he's looking good. He's upped the stakes! He was the musical director for Sarah Blasko when she toured here. So his currency is rising in some of these circles - he's connected to the pop world too. I can see him doing more of that work.

"Did you know he grew up with and loved Doris Day! That made me laugh. When I was a kid I was always interested in the Eurovision Song Contest - it's like a sort of Olympic Games of entertainment. He amazed me when he said he always enjoyed watching Eurovision, and ever since we've watched it together. We really listen to the songs and we've become quite expert about who's going to win. He's got that sensibility for all musical genres. That's what keeps him current and across everything.

"He's an influencer. He's influenced a whole generation of young music people and inspired them. He gives so much: he's a mentor for so many people in different ways."

Dolomites, 2019 (Courtesy, Florian Peelman)

The future
WHAT NEXT?

The future for any musician in a post pandemic world looks grim. Cultural industries provide enormous economic benefit to the nation, vastly disproportionate to the remuneration of artists ands arts workers. But during the pandemic, the dominant 'gig' based employment of arts workers vanished overnight.

He finds it heartbreaking to see artists lose work, livelihood – and our concert halls empty. On the other hand, he sees it as a fact of life that artists in general work for far below what people consider proper rates. The amount of personal preparation and commitment to craft is rarely quantified or remunerated. He says: "I suspect that artists take this in their stride and use this time to take stock, learn something new, plan new projects, do the things that never get done.... There is a silver lining to every cloud."

As director of a growing but precariously low-funded festival, Roland Peelman is realistic about the harsh prospects for his festival but is determined to proceed with the artistic priorities defined in conjunction with the CIMF Board. In the early weeks of the pandemic when the 2020 Festival was cancelled, it was touch and go whether the organisation would survive. His resourceful response was to create a virtual online festival during the weeks of the cancelled festival, streamed from actual daily performances. He says it was "frustrating to let go of everything we worked on for more than a year, and why I call it 'the best festival we never had.' On the other hand, our commitments to new work remain in place and many of the 2020 festival artists and projects will find their way into the next festivals."

Apart from severe financial constraints, the Festival in Canberra allows him almost complete free rein in choosing what he wants to present and what he himself directs. It offers him endless opportunity for musical engagement that fascinates him and allows him to present audiences with new and exciting experiences.

Of course it can't go on forever: he has another four years on his contract. Would he want to move on to one of Australia's larger festivals? Most of them: such as Sydney, Melbourne, Adelaide or Perth Festivals consist primarily of a conglomeration of bought-in events, largely from overseas festival circuits. It seems likely he would find this unchallenging, even boring.

Many music lovers regard his twenty-five years patient building of The Song Company into a world-leading vocal ensemble as his finest achievement. The sudden end of the ensemble of singers in 2019 is widely seen as a tragedy for Australian music. Some have expressed the hope he will lead a new vocal ensemble in due course. It is unlikely. His departure in 2015 was carefully considered, as he felt he needed new challenges. No doubt he would advise or support establishment of a new ensemble if it involved suitable leadership and singers.

The option of going back to Europe where his special talents would be highly appreciated, seems unlikeliest of all. Virtually his whole career has been in Australia. He loves Australia. He has engaged so completely and so generously with the Australian musical scene. Australian Indigenous music and culture is a huge commitment for him. Most of all, three of his children either live or spend large parts of their lives here; his eldest Jozefien, is hoping to come with her family to Australia to live.

It is clear there are few if any people to facilitate change at all levels to music in Australia with such insight and drive as Roland Peelman. A quick glance at the status and health of music as an industry is not reassuring. Apart from some elite tertiary music institutions, music education, especially in terms of trained teachers in public schools, is almost non-existent; most performing organisations, orchestras, opera, choirs, ensembles are desperately underfunded; even the popular music industry is in the doldrums. Restoring musical health in Australia in the aftermath of the pandemic will be a huge challenge for our musical leadership. Roland's life as a performer is so rich and varied that he may never be tempted to take on a more political role as a cultural leader.

However, there is no doubt he has the knowledge and temperament for it and, in the right position, the country would benefit.

Appendix

Composer commissions initiated by Roland Peelman

In the thirty years since he was engaged by The Song Company in 1990, Roland Peelman has been responsible for commissioning, either directly or through another commissioning body, 164 new works of music from a total of 85 composers.

This astonishing and sustained initiative by a single musician is unprecedented in Australia and possibly anywhere. Most of the composers are Australian but many are from other countries such as New Zealand, USA, China, Hong Kong, Philippines, Malaysia, Singapore, Belgium, UK, Denmark and Mexico.

Most of these works have been performed, sometimes many times, by artists, ensembles, even opera companies, in Australia and abroad under the direction of Roland Peelman and other musicians. They range over the whole gamut of musical styles and forms, from songs or short instrumental pieces of a few minutes' length to operas, music theatre, or orchestral works of an hour or more in duration.

The composers who have been commissioned are set out below. For further details of the works commissioned, contact the writer at antony@antonyjeffrey.com, or Roland Peelman at info@cimf.org.au

Katy Abbott
Stephen Adams
Simon Barker
Jodie Blackshaw
Jack Body (NZ)
Anne Boyd
Colin Bright
Gerard Brophy
Nigel Butterley
Guido Castanogli (IT)
Eve de Castro-Robinson
Hing-yan Chan (HK)
Lyle Chan
Alice Chance
Tristan Coelho
Lisa Crane
Stephen Cronin
Olivia Bettina Davies
Michael Dooley
Ben Drury
Ross Edwards
Gareth Farr (NZ)
Many Finsterer
Jacqueline Fontyn (BE)
Andrew Ford
Jennifer Fowler
Brenda Gifford
Jess Green
Stuart Greenbaum
Andrée Greenwell
Pelle Gudmundson-Holmgreen (DK)
Holly Harrison
Matthew Hindson
Moya Henderson
Brian Howard
Paul Jarman
Elena Kats-Chernin
Joyce Bee Tuan Koh (SG)

Konstantine Koukias
Bun-ching Lam (US)
Liza Lim
David Lumsdaine
Ella Macens
Ray Marcellino
Ruth McCall
Kate Neal
Nicholas Ng
Frank Nuyts (BE)
Rosalind Page
Anna Pimakhova
Alex Pozniak
Qin Yi (CH)
Bree van Reyk
Damien Ricketson
Saidah Rastam (MY)
Chris Sainsbury
Andrew Schultz
Veronique Serret & William Barton
Na-lin Shen (CH)
Lachlan Skipworth
Caroline Szeto
Hollis Taylor
Alessandro Timossi (IT)
Mark Viggiani
James Wade
Nick Wales
Juan Felipe Waller (MEX)
Jessica Wells
Martin Wesley-Smith
Sally Whitwell
Gillian Whitehead (NZ)
Michael Whiticker
Julian Yu

Anthony Browell

Anthony lives in Sydney, and has spent a life in and out of photography. Working in portraiture, advertising, editorial, architectural as well as personal photography, has enabled him to experience being around a wide variety of amazing and talented people. Recently this has included musicians of many genres.

His other interests include inland paddle-steamers of Australia, his family, and large format pinhole cameras.

Antony Jeffrey

Antony Jeffrey has enjoyed a long career in the arts. He was the first director of the Australia Council Music Board, and first general manager of the Australian Chamber Orchestra. He has worked in senior roles for many other arts companies and in the corporate sector.

He has recorded over 100 interviews with artists and people associated with the arts, many of which resulted in his book Many Faces of Inspiration (2011). These days he organises and leads music tours abroad as well as indulging in writing when he has time.

"I have a problem with institutions and become very impatient with their mindsets, and it shows. It says something about who I am. When I was young, I had a problem with school and I had a problem with the Church and later with government! I fared well in organisations that were not institutionalised. I think that explains why I did well at The Song Company because I made it work at a personal level and avoided the bureaucracy of an institution."

Roland Peelman

www.ingramcontent.com/pod-product-compliance
Lightning Source LLC
Chambersburg PA
CBHW040842100426
42812CB00014B/2588